ENGLISH ▦ HERITAGE

Book of
Dartmoor
Landscapes through time

Sandy Gerrard

B. T. Batsford / English Heritage
London

© Sandy Gerrard 1997

First published 1997

All rights reserved. No part of this publication
may be reproduced in any form or by any means,
without permission from the Publisher.

Typeset by Bernard Cavender Design & Greenwood Graphics Publishing
Printed and bound by The Bath Press, Bath

Published by B.T. Batsford Ltd
583 Fulham Road, London SW6 5BY

A CIP catalogue record for this book is
available from the British Library

ISBN 0 7134 7589 7

(*Front cover*) A view of Grimspound from Hameldown Tor
(© *British Tourist Authority Photo Library*)

Contents

Illustrations

Colour plates

Tables

Acknowledgements

I have many people to thank for helping me produce this book, and without whom it would never have appeared in its present form. Technical data, photographs, illustrations and reasoned debate have been provided by David Austin, Shirley Blaylock, Jeremy Butler, Debbie Griffiths, Philip Newman, Chris Powell, Paul Rendell, John Schofield and Tess Walker. Special thanks are owed to Frances Griffith and her staff at Devon County Council for allowing me extensive use of the Devon Sites and Monuments Register (SMR), which must represent the most comprehensive source of archaeological information relating to the moor.

I owe a special debt to those – including Frances Griffith, Dave Hooley, Mark Patton, Chris Reaney, Paul Rendell and Julian Richards – who generously read through my fevered ponderings and mindless irreverences to the English language, and who, despite this, are still speaking to me. The fabulous reconstruction drawings which have brought aspects of the past to life are all due to Chris Powell.

Thanks are also gratefully acknowledged for the help provided by Anne Dunbar-Nobes (copy editor), Monica Kendall and Charlotte Vickerstaff of Batsford for the care they have taken in seeing the book through the various stages to its present state. To my greatest critic – my daughter Iona – who, at a very tender age and on several occasions, gave vent to her feelings about my work by trying to eat the typescript or deleting great chunks of it on the computer – I can say 'OK, we'll play ball now, I've finished!' and actually mean it.

Without doubt I am most indebted to Helen, my wife, who tolerated being a 'book widow' and continually offered much needed support and willingness to search for original approaches to thorny issues. For all this and the occasional touches of inspired genius I dedicate the result with gratitude.

Preface

Dartmoor's landscape is the product of millennia of human interference. The vast expanse of high moorland is the direct result of early widespread forest clearance, unwittingly leading to the development of the blanket bog which survives to this day. On the lower slopes more intensive agricultural activity in both prehistoric and historic times is witnessed by the widespread survival of relict field-systems and settlements. In the valley bottoms large areas have been turned upside down producing undulations indicative of ancient tin extraction. Elsewhere the patchwork of present day fields, most of which were originally brought into cultivation thousands of years ago, emphasizes the continuing importance of agriculture to this upland economy.

At the very heart of Devon, in south-west England, the rocky tors of Dartmoor loom broodingly over the surrounding countryside, frequently bathed in ethereal mists which make them seem mountainous and mysterious (**1**). Anyone, who either knows or has heard about Dartmoor, will have their very own personal images and feelings for the place, which will be as varied as the landscape itself. Dartmoor has much to offer and among its riches is a particularly well-preserved archaeological landscape which is both informative and largely accessible. Our knowledge of Dartmoor's archaeology has been built up by the hard work, diligent observations and research of a large number of antiquarians and archaeologists over a period of several generations. The aim of this book is to

gather together and present the results of their endeavours. Archaeology has always been somewhat subjective; consequently, over the years, the interpretations by various individuals, even of the same material, has produced a plethora of hypotheses varying in emphasis and direction. As a result there can never be a definitive account of Dartmoor's history as revealed by its landscape. This may strike a rather pessimistic note, but I consider it refreshing to know that future discoveries and attitudes will inevitably lead us all to re-examine our own ideas about the landscape and the way in which it has evolved.

In addition to the information visible to the eye, there is a great deal more buried below the surface. Excavations over the past 150 years have considerably enhanced our understanding of the function, date and character of the many different types of monument. Another source of information has been the examination of environmental data which has indicated the changing character of the vegetation. In the historic period, documents provide a glimpse into the past and form another useful source of information. Together these enhance the accuracy of our understanding of the development in land-use.

Dartmoor is an extremely difficult area to delimit, and though criteria including geology, climate, altitude, topography, vegetation and land-use have been utilized in the past, no single boundary has been accepted. In 1951, Dartmoor was designated as a National Park and for the first time a boundary line was drawn and signs

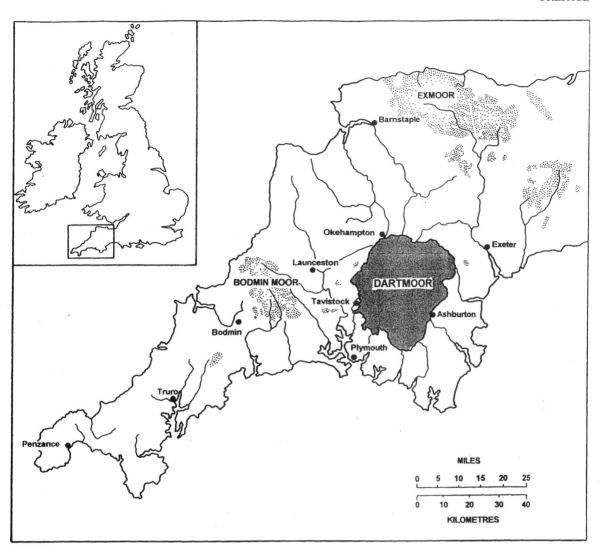

erected (**2**). The area defined by the National Park includes a wide diversity of existing landscape types including high moorland, high farmland, fringe farmland, woodland, forestry, villages and towns (**3**). In the public imagination the area designated as National Park is now thought of as Dartmoor and for this reason this book will examine the archaeological landscape within this modern administrative area, with one significant addition. The moorland around Crownhill Down immediately south of the Park will be considered as part of the moor because in antiquity it formed part of the overall pattern of upland exploitation.

An archaeological landscape contains all aspects of human activity which leave tangible

1 *Location map: Britain and the south-western peninsula.*

remains. Imagine a sandy beach, early in the morning just after the high tide, homogeneous and bare. A man walks his dog leaving footprints; children play, drawing shapes one over another, building sand castles and dams; items are buried or lost, litter accumulates. By the evening we see a confused pattern of activity, which bears witness to the history of a day. In a similar way landscape patterns develop through time. In order to make sense of the apparent chaos, archaeologists produce chronological frameworks of 'what happened when'. This involves peeling back layers of time and concluding which events and their

11

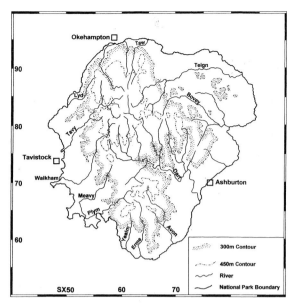

2 *Much of Dartmoor lies above 300m and this has contributed a great deal to the creation and survival of this unique archaeological landscape. Most of the surviving visible prehistoric archaeology is found between the 300m and 450m contours. The inner border represents the National Park boundary as redefined in 1994.*

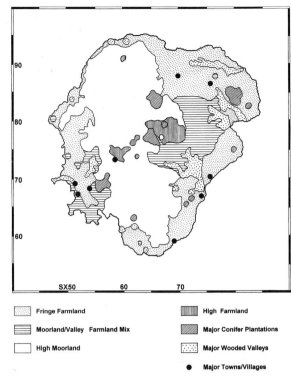

3 *Current land-use within the National Park. This illustration highlights the major differences in current land-use. It is crucial to consider current land-use when examining the meaning of archaeological distributions. In particular, flint scatters are generally more likely to come from farmland under the plough while well-preserved earthworks are more likely to survive in moorland. (After Atkinson 1991.)*

resultant landforms are broadly contiguous. In some instances, science has enabled exact dates to be ascertained.

There are very few radiocarbon dates from Dartmoor and this makes absolute dating of the monuments difficult. Generally, parallels with similar sites for which dating is available are used to provide a chronological framework. The use of the traditional terminology to describe the major periods of prehistory is necessary because of the shortage of absolute dating evidence. Clearly, however, there is considerable overlap with particular types of monument being built and used in more than one period.

The spelling of Dartmoor place names has varied over the years, with many places having several different forms. The Ordnance Survey has attempted to standardize these, and in the process has alienated those who prefer the older forms. Unless otherwise indicated the place-name spellings used are those shown on the Ordnance Survey maps, as this should make it easier for the reader to locate the sites referred to.

1
Reading the landscape: sources of information

Introduction

Dartmoor contains a fascinating diversity of important archaeological sites illustrating many facets of human history. It represents one of the best preserved and most complete upland archaeological landscapes in Britain. Evidence of settlements, sepulchral monuments, ritual sites, agricultural and industrial activity can be seen throughout the area. Dartmoor was first exploited by hunters and gatherers during the Palaeolithic and Mesolithic periods, though no structures are known to date from this time. The earliest visible structures probably date to the Neolithic and may include at least two hilltop enclosures, together with a number of stone rows and burial cairns. The prehistoric archaeology for which the upland moor is best known, however, belongs to the Bronze Age. At this time, the moor was densely settled by people whose homes, fields, burial places and religious centres still survive and may be appreciated by both visitor and archaeologist alike. The different components of the Bronze Age landscape have in places remained unaltered since they were abandoned over 2600 years ago. In many areas, however, later generations have developed and altered the earlier features to meet their own specific requirements. The result of this later activity is often a landscape containing a complex array of interrelated and different archaeological features belonging to several periods of activity (**colour plate 1**).

This type of archaeological landscape is best described as a palimpsest, like an 'old master', where the canvas has been reused several times, but older images still survive beneath newer veneers of paint. The palimpsest is especially informative as it allows us to see each generation reacting to the landscape left by the previous one. Examples of palimpsests are abundant throughout the moor and, in many areas, structures belonging to the Bronze Age, medieval and post-medieval periods are found together in close proximity (**4**). Palimpsest landscapes are often both complex and confusing when seen for the first time and it is essential to their comprehension that the different components are accurately identified and understood. In general, a proper understanding of a complex landscape is only possible if all the available information is recorded and available for analysis.

On Dartmoor, field survey is considered to be the best non-destructive way in which to untangle the complex and often confusing web of earthworks and other structures. Such survey involves the production of detailed plans showing the precise position, character, relationship and interpretation of the different features. Once the information is transferred from the field onto a plan it is much easier to understand the archaeological details and the sequence in which they were constructed. Interpretation based on survey information can be presented to both an academic and wider audience for scrutiny and re-interpretation.

Archaeological survey has been carried out by a large number of individuals and organizations,

4 *The Vag Hill palimpsest. Much of Vag Hill enclosed by prehistoric rectangular fields was brought back into cultivation during the medieval period when some of the earlier boundaries were rebuilt and slight ridges formed as a result of ploughing. Later still, in the post medieval period, rectangular mounds known as pillow mounds and X-shaped vermin traps were constructed to serve a rabbit warren. (Photograph Frances Griffith, Devon County Council: copyright reserved.)*

although unfortunately much of it has been either monument specific or has excluded certain elements of the palimpsest. The first known detailed archaeological field survey was carried out at the prehistoric settlement, stone rows and cairns at Merrivale by Colonel Hamilton Smith in 1828. In the latter part of the nineteenth century, the Dartmoor Exploration Committee, appreciating the need for plans of the sites they investigated, produced a number of plans including those of sites at Grimspound, Langstone Moor, Standon Down and Watern Oke. Throughout the twentieth century a large number of individuals and organizations have carried out field surveys.

The two most comprehensive archaeological surveys of the moor are both based on aerial photographs. In 1985, the Royal Commission for Historic Monuments (England) produced an archaeological map using information from aerial

14

photographs. The second survey was carried out by Butler, who followed up his aerial photographic work with a programme of field checking. This has resulted in the first readily accessible plans showing the complexity of Dartmoor's archaeology.

Several more detailed surveys of more limited geographical extent have been carried out during the past thirty years and among these are Kestor by Fox, the Dartmeet coaxial field-system by Fleming, the Upper Plym valley by Mercer, and Okehampton Park by Austin and Daggett. Finally, the Ordnance Survey and, latterly, the Royal Commission for Historic Monuments (England) have surveyed and interpreted a large number of individual monuments and blocks of relict landscape.

Many archaeologists have considerably enhanced our understanding and appreciation of individual structures with their detailed surveys of individual monuments. Among those which deserve special mention are Worth's and Haynes' surveys of various different types of deserted buildings, Turner's work on ring cairns and Butler's surveys of many different classes of monument.

Excavation

Archaeological investigation has not been limited to survey; for over a century, excavations have been adding to our knowledge of the area. The earliest 'digging' activity was unfortunately not for information but rather for treasure, and sadly the result of this episode of interest in the prehistoric burial cairns was the loss without record of important archaeological information.

At least 92 per cent of the recorded cairns have been damaged at some time by this type of activity, though because of an obsessive interest in the central burial, much important information does remain. The cairns which have been damaged in this way can be identified by the hollow in the centre of the mound which is usually circular in shape (5). Probably the earliest excavation for which information is recorded was that carried out by Hannaford in 1827. He opened a cist on the eastern slopes of Higher White Tor and found human hair. These early excavations are

5 *The large pit dug into the centre of this cairn (situated just below the summit of Yes Tor) clearly indicates that even the most remote of cairns were the victims of robbers. (Author.)*

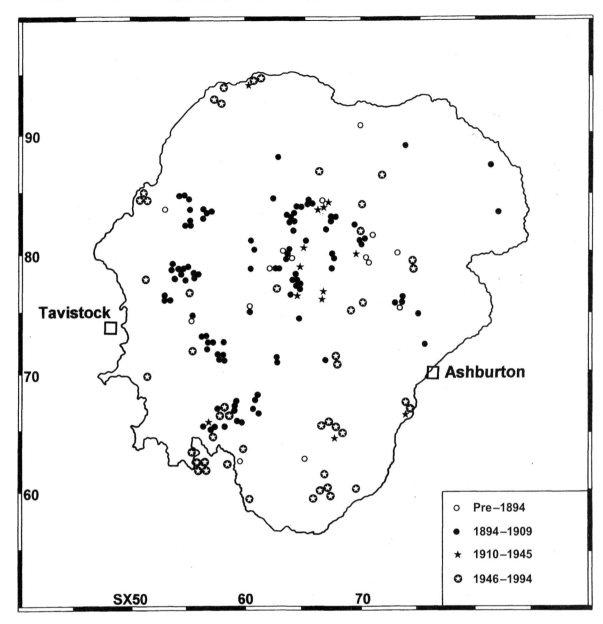

considered by modern scholars to have been inadequate as often the details given are very sketchy and the techniques very primitive. The first concerted attempt at understanding Dartmoor's past through excavation was the work of the Dartmoor Exploration Committee. Between 1894 and 1905 it carried out a large number of excavations on a diverse range of sites in different parts of the moor (6). The quality of the information generated from this work varies considerably. On occasion, there is only a passing reference to the excavation of a site, while at other times, details of finds and structures are given. At the large-scale excavation of the prehistoric settlement at Watern Oke in 1905, ninety-four prehistoric round houses were excavated by eight people in the course of eight weeks! This represents an average of about two houses per day and emphasizes the fundamental difference between their excavation techniques and those of the present, when a project of this scale would necessarily take several years and

6 *Distribution of Dartmoor excavations. This map illustrates clearly the different excavation strategies of successive generations. Before 1894, there were few documented excavations and they appear to be randomly distributed. In the following period the work of the Dartmoor Exploration Committee and the Barrow Committee form the majority of the work and with few exceptions they appear to be confined to the high moorland. The period up until the end of the Second World War saw relatively little activity. The excavations carried out since 1945 generally cluster around the edges of the moor and many represent 'rescue excavations' carried out in advance of destruction by roads, reservoirs, farming and the china-clay industry. (Source: Devon SMR.)*

cost much more than the limited resources available to a local research organization. Despite the obvious limitations, the excavation work carried out by the Committee remains the largest single body of excavated evidence from the moor, and recent work by Marchant has clearly demonstrated that the Committee's contribution to our understanding of the moor's archaeology has been seriously underestimated and that its work still has a great deal to offer the modern scholar.

Excavations by Lady Fox at the prehistoric settlements at Kestor and Dean Moor represent the first carried out under more rigorous and structured conditions. Important details concerning the dating and economic character of this type of settlement were derived from her work, which confirmed some earlier conclusions about their character. In recent years a large number of excavations have been undertaken at a variety of locations and site types. These include the round houses and land-division boundaries at Holne Moor by Fleming (**7**); an enclosed settlement, cairns and field-systems at Shaugh Moor by Wainwright; Gibson's excavation of a prehistoric settlement at Gold Park on Shapley Moor; excavation of a deserted medieval farmstead within Okehampton Park by Austin; Minter's work at the medieval settlements of Hound Tor, Hutholes and Dinna Clerks, together with the prehistoric settlement on Heatree Down; excavations in advance of the Okehampton bypass by English

Heritage and the Exeter Museums Archaeological Field Unit, who have also re-examined one of the buildings at Hutholes (**colour plate 2**); and the Dartmoor Tinworking Research Group at a post-medieval tin-smelting mill near Merrivale. These excavations and others have contributed much information to our understanding of the different types of site and the results inevitably form a significant part of our appreciation of the moor's archaeology.

Survey and excavation are not the only tools available to the archaeologist. Information concerning the changing environment of the area survives in a number of locations and has been collected, analysed and interpreted to provide an environmental background and explanation for many of the recognized human activities detected by other archaeological means. Much of the environmental work in the area has been concerned with establishing the vegetational history. This has been achieved using pollen analysis. Each

7 *Excavated round houses on Holne Moor. Excavations within the larger round house revealed a complex developmental history including the two major prehistoric stone buildings shown here and a recent shelter. The smaller building was constructed within the ruins of the larger house. (Andrew Fleming: copyright reserved.)*

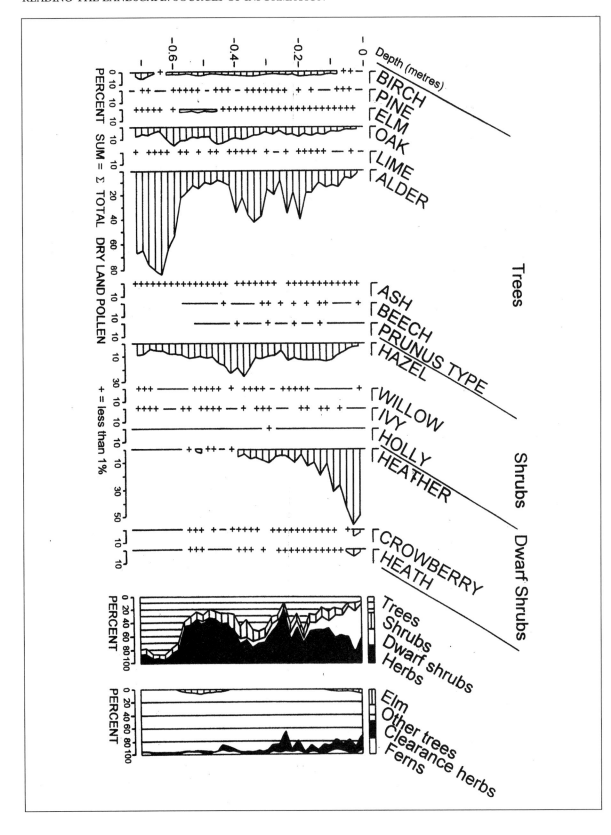

8 *A specimen pollen diagram showing how the relative quantity of different plant species varied through time. The oldest deposits are at the bottom and the youngest at the top. Note how the tree cover, particularly alder, has declined while heather has increased. (After Beckett 1981.)*

year, pollen is produced by trees and plants and carried in the wind. Much of this pollen falls to the ground and, on Dartmoor, the pollen that comes to rest in the peat has been preserved in this acid and anaerobic (oxygen-free) environment. Over hundreds and thousands of years successive layers of pollen have been incorporated into the developing peat deposits. By examining in detail the pollen from each layer, variations over time in the local vegetation can be identified. The information from pollen analysis is generally expressed most easily in a bar-chart called a pollen diagram (**8**). The earliest analysis of pollen on the moor was carried out in the 1960s by Simmons who successfully built up a general vegetational history of the area. In recent years, further work by Caseldine and Hatton has considerably refined the picture and provided absolute dates for many of the events using radiocarbon dating. Most of the excavation programmes completed within the past two decades have contained a palaeo-environmental element and the results of this work have provided complementary information which has considerably enhanced the interpretation.

Within the same peat bogs remains of tree stumps, branches and seeds are known to survive, but perhaps because of the richness of the pollen data, little work has been carried out on this potentially useful source of information. However, the same conditions which have preserved the pollen and other vegetable matter so well means that other sources of environmental information are not available to the Dartmoor scholar. Bone in particular does not survive in the acid soils; thus, the detailed analyses of faunal remains which have proved so informative in other parts of southern England have no place here. Likewise snail shells, which provide vital information on the vegetation at many sites, do not survive. Soil analysis, and in particular examination of phosphate levels, has been successfully used at several sites to examine patterns of human and animal activity. Animal manure is rich in phosphate, which when released into the soil below becomes permanently fixed by being bonded with aluminium and iron compounds. By analysing phosphate levels within the soil it is possible to find the location and extent of areas where animal and human manure was deposited. At Shaugh Moor it was possible to demonstrate that the enclosure around the earlier settlement was probably built to exclude animals from the settlement rather than to protect them because phosphate levels within the enclosure were generally low (**9**).

One important source of information which complements our understanding of the historic landscape is contemporary documentation. From the Early Christian period a trickle of documents builds into a flood by the nineteenth century. The types of documentation are varied, some being clearly more useful than others, but together they form an extremely important source of information concerning land-use, agricultural and industrial practices, manorial and industrial customs and laws.

Information gleaned from all this archaeological work is held in two separate places. The first is the National Archaeological Record (NAR), which holds information on a computerized database covering the whole of England. Each monument has been assigned its own unique reference number based on the 1:10,000 Ordnance Survey map series. Detailed descriptions of many monuments together with survey information and photographs are kept at their offices in Swindon. The second repository is the Devon County Sites and Monuments Register (SMR) which is held at County Hall in Exeter. This database contains information of the same kind as the NAR, and is the most complete record of Devon's archaeology. Its primary purpose is as a conservation tool, but it is also an excellent and readily available source of information concerning all aspects of Devon's archaeological heritage.

9 *Excavated enclosure on Shaugh Moor. This enclosure appears to have been built to prevent livestock entering the settlement. Other examples, by contrast, may have been built to provide protection for animals. (City of Plymouth Museum and Art Gallery: copyright reserved.)*

The SMR is the most complete and up-to-date source of information concerning Dartmoor's archaeological landscape, and it has therefore been used extensively in preparing this book.

Dartmoor contains a wide variety of monument types which together form the complex palimpsest for which the moor is known. Each generation of moorland people has left its imprint on the landscape for the archaeologist to record, interpret and (on occasion) understand. Field survey and excavation have provided a body of information from which archaeologists have been able to analyse the way in which different parts of the moor have developed through time to meet different cultural, social, economic and climatic conditions. Each area of the moor bears witness to several major periods of activity and contains a variety of monuments together forming the important and informative

landscape. This book is for the most part arranged in a chronological sequence, in order to allow a picture of the character and extent of each major period's impact on the landscape to be assessed more easily, but such an approach masks the way in which particular groups of geographically related sites evolved to form the landscape visible today. The final chapter, therefore, examines a few selected examples of palimpsests and illustrates the way in which careful study can be used to unravel the developing picture.

The archaeology of the moor, in common with other areas of the country, has been examined in a piecemeal manner. Different scholars have selected separate parts of the landscape to answer specific questions of interest to them – there has been no single attempt to draw all these archaeological strands together and to investigate the total picture of human interaction on Dartmoor. The early cairn diggers were concerned only with the contents of the central grave. The antiquarians were again primarily interested in the contents and character of the burials under the cairns they were investigating, though this time their search was motivated by the search for knowledge rather than treasure. The same anti-quarians were also interested in the living places of those interred in the nearby cairns and set about excavating a large number of houses and surveying a small number of settlements. At no time did they direct their attentions to excavating the associated fields although in some cases they did produce plans of them.

In recent years the same basic approach of examining a single element or strand of the land-scape has been repeated, generally for reasons of economy, practicality or because the individuals involved were driven by a specific research inter-est. It is unwise to be overly critical of such an approach since any complete archaeological land-scape study has to start somewhere. Even under ideal conditions, a complete study of all the rami-fications of the complex archaeological landscape would take an eternity. This at a time when not all of the different types of monument present are fully understood. A first priority in the develop-ment of an appreciation of the landscape as a whole is an understanding of the different compo-nents. Much work has been carried out, as witnessed by the several hundred academic arti-cles and scores of books, but compared with the extent of the area and complexity of the archaeol-ogy, the existing database is incomplete. I challenge anyone armed with a copy of the plans in this book or any other to go out onto Dartmoor and not find something of interest which has not previously been recorded. In some instances the discovery may simply enhance and confirm our understanding of the area, but on other occasions it may call for a rethink of a sig-nificant part of the existing interpretation. For me, this is one of the greatest pleasures of visiting archaeological sites on the moor; you can visit the same area time after time and on each occasion fresh discoveries can lead one to rethink and eval-uate previous ideas. I would, therefore, expect and sincerely hope that future survey and research projects and even casual visits will improve our knowledge and ultimately our under-standing of the moor's archaeology.

Components in the landscape

Archaeologists examining a complex landscape such as Dartmoor need to be able to describe it in a way which makes sense to other archaeologists and interested visitors alike. The easiest way in which this can be achieved is to give specific names to the same types of feature. In purely objective terms, the Dartmoor landscape includes a complex series of walls, banks, mounds, ditches, hollows, pits and stones, which the archaeologist has to resolve into different types of archaeologi-cal feature. This exercise is not as straightforward as one might think. The archaeological literature is full of examples of sites which have at different times been interpreted quite differently. On Dartmoor, the most quoted case is of the crom-lech at Merrivale that still survives within one of the enclosures but which is now known to be an apple-crusher stone (**10**). In the same vicinity, the pillow mounds belonging to the rabbit warren were identified by the Rev. Bray in 1832 as prehis-toric burial mounds, and small trenches cut into the side of some of these mounds bear physical testimony to this belief. These mis-identifications may seem amusing viewed from the present but they do emphasize a real problem faced by archaeologists today. How does one know for sure that the label one has attached to a particular site or group of features is the correct one, and how does one know from surface indications only what exactly lies below the ground? The truth is that we cannot be sure, although comparison with other excavated and surveyed sites does make the interpretation more reliable.

Some types of monument are more difficult to identify in the field than others and the diligent visitor must look for the clues which will indicate the most likely interpretation. In many cases, however, there is just enough surviving evidence to allow a particular identification to be reached and in these instances the reasons for favouring one particular answer over another must be justi-fied. Many sites fall into this category and some have had their identity changed as further field-work has suggested fresh interpretations. On the slopes of Cox Tor and Mis Tor, for example, a

10 *This apple-crusher stone, propped up awaiting transportation, was once mistaken for a cromlech (chambered tomb). Such stones were used to crush apples as part of the process of making cider. (Author.)*

large number of 'hut circles' are shown on recent Ordnance Survey maps, but in the field, the walls look too fresh and in every instance each of these structures is accompanied by at least three small rectangular pits. For these reasons doubt has been expressed concerning the identity of these structures. Examination of aerial photographs taken in 1946 confirmed that these structures were of recent origin. At the moment these structures are accepted as circular platforms built during mortar training in the Second World War, but further work may mean a fresh interpretation is reached. Similar structures survive at Shavercombe, where the picture is further complicated by their association with a number of genuine round houses. Here, however we are fortunate in that three examples clearly cut an existing medieval boundary bank thus proving that they cannot be of prehistoric date. Identification problems are so common that it is useful to highlight those types of site which are known to have caused problems (**Table 1**).

Identification of particular monuments is, to a certain extent, dependent on the expertise and experience of the archaeologist, and some of the identifications presented here will certainly be challenged and reviewed in the years to come. To confuse the picture further archaeologists often define classes of monuments in slightly different ways, the result being that the same site can be called by a number of different terms although everyone may agree on what survives. Thus, for example, the Nine Stones on Belstone Common is variously described as a cairn circle and a stone circle; similarly, tin-stamping mills are often referred to as blowing houses. Having established that identification of the different types of archaeological site is necessarily subjective, we should not be surprised to discover the impact this has on the way in which we interpret the landscape formed by these different features.

To aid understanding of the different types of monuments, archaeologists generate typologies designed to highlight and allow examination of differences between examples of the same type of site. A recent published example relates to cairns containing visible stone rings, but others exist for many types of site including prehistoric round houses, settlements, stone rows and tinworks.

Dartmoor's archaeological landscape can be seen and examined in a number of different ways. For the purposes of this book the character and nature of each major period is examined separately to allow an overview of their contribution to the Dartmoor palimpsest. There are, however, common threads which run through most of the major periods.

FIELD EVIDENCE	POSSIBLE INTERPRETATIONS
Linear stone and earth bank	Dam : field boundary : leat Railway or road embankment Reave : spoil dump
Linear stone and earth bank with ditch	Leat : drainage ditch Field boundary : vermin trap
Circular bank surrounding a level internal area with a diameter of less than 12m	Animal pound : beehive hut : buddle (circular) Charcoal burner's hearth Military mortar emplacement Ring cairn : robbed round cairn : round house Shelter : tinners' building
Earthwork enclosing a large internal area	Enclosure : field : hillfort Hilltop enclosure
Circular mound	Beacon : clearance cairn : motte Natural mound : peat stack : pillow mound Round cairn : spoil dump
Circular or oval pit	Bomb crater : lode-back pit Prospecting pit : sawpit : shaft Well
Large pit or hollow	Claypit : mill pond : pond Quarry : reservoir : sandpit
Rectangular building (with leat)	Blowing mill : corn mill Crazing mill : stamping mill Woollen mill
Alignment of upright stones	Clitter : field boundary : stone row
Rectangular earthwork	Barn : buddle (rectangular) : chapel Icework : longhouse : peat cutting Shelter
Linear hollow	Corn ditch : drainage gully : openwork Holloway : natural hollow
Long mound	Long cairn : pillow mound
Hole leading into hillside	Adit : hull : tunnel
Solitary upright stone	Boundary stone : cross (damaged) Memorial stone : milestone : route marker Rubbing stone : standing stone
A circle of stones	Circular enclosure : kerbed cairn Round house : ring cairn : stone circle
Several mounds lying within close proximity	Cairnfield : cairn cemetery : warren
Stone with hollows in its surface	Cup-marked stone : mortar stone

Table 1 *Problems of archaeological interpretation in the field. This list is by no means exhaustive and is intended to illustrate a selection of the different possible interpretations from similar field evidence. Association of different features is always an important criterion in reaching a plausible interpretation.*

2

Hunter-gatherers to the first farmers: early modifications to the natural landscape

Palaeolithic (c. 350,000–10,000 BC)

The information concerning the character of settlement and exploitation during this period comes largely from environmental evidence, a relatively small number of stray finds and cave sites several miles east of the moor. During this time, Britain was joined to mainland Europe and research indicates that the continent was exploited by bands of hunters and gatherers who migrated with their prey and lived a nomadic existence, establishing ephemeral campsites. In Devon, the earliest known site at Kent's Cavern may date to the latter part of the Cromerian Interglacial or to a warmer interlude in the Anglian Glaciation (c. 350,000–250,000 BC). Such 'precise' dating of the remaining Lower Palaeolithic artefacts is impossible though many probably belong to the later Hoxnian Interglacial, Wolstonian Glaciation and Ipswichian Interglacial (c. 250,000–70,000 BC). Large numbers of generally unstratified Lower Palaeolithic flint tools have been found in Devon, but only two find spots are of special interest to Dartmoor. The first of these is at Tavistock where eleven handaxes and at least two flakes were found, which certainly indicates some activity at this time around the fringe of the moor. The second and arguably more interesting artefact is the flint implement of Palaeolithic type found on Brent Moor by Worth in 1931. If this flint is accepted at face value it would appear to support the idea that Dartmoor was first exploited during the Lower Palaeolithic.

During the Early Upper Palaeolithic period, Devon appears only to have been occupied during the summer months by small groups of people following and hunting herds of reindeer. They lived in caves and probably on open sites around Torbay and the Plymouth area. If the reindeer ever ventured onto Dartmoor it is almost certain they would have been followed, but sadly there is no evidence to support this.

During the Late Upper Palaeolithic, the severe weather conditions of the Devensian Glaciation (from about 16,000 to 13,000 BC) meant that Devon was probably unpopulated. Following the warming after this glaciation, the climate rapidly improved and by 11,000 BC open grassland followed by patches of birch woodland had colonized nearby Bodmin Moor. Again the caves at Kent's Cavern were occupied, though now birds and smaller mammals were also eaten together with wild horse, deer and bear.

Mesolithic (c. 10,000–4500 BC)

Although the use of the moor during the Palaeolithic has yet to be proven beyond reasonable doubt, it is known with certainty that the area was exploited during the Mesolithic. This period is distinguished from the earlier one by the development of the production of differing types of flint tool, together with the development of different patterns of subsistence in response to warming climatic conditions. No early Mesolithic flints have yet been found on Dartmoor, although this is more likely a result of a failure to locate the sites rather than any absence of activity. On nearby Bodmin Moor a substantial number of flints have been recovered from Dozmary Pool and other sites. The first tangible archaeological evidence for exploitation of the moor belongs to the later Mesolithic, when a number of sites producing large quantities of the characteristic flint blades have been found.

Sites which have produced characteristic Mesolithic flints include Batworthy, Gidleigh Common, East Week and, buried beneath peat, Ringhill in the Stannon Brook. A number of sites must still lie buried below the deep blanket-peat deposits, which denote the favourable upland hunting grounds. Because they have been protected, traces of shelters and other associated structures, similar to those found at some of the coastal sites in Devon, may survive remarkably well.

Flint tools in the Mesolithic were utilized for a variety of purposes. There were scrapers and borers of various sizes, burins and flakes. Microliths are common. These are tiny blades made from long flints and often geometrically shaped, designed to be mounted as boring and cutting tools. Singly they were used to produce points for bone arrows and fish hooks. Many were also mounted together in wooden handles to produce cutting edges, and all were used for hunting, fishing and gathering. Burins and boring tools could be used to make bone and antler implements such as needles. Consequently, we can infer the production of leather and hide goods, clothes, bags, cups and so forth.

By studying microliths we can infer a little about the lives of the moorland people. Flint scatters, like those at Langstone Moor where a knapping site produced 441 worked flints and flakes in a roughly circular heap, automatically leads us to imagine an individual or a group of people sitting and spending a few hours creating tools for hunting trips, amid the usual social chatter. The litter of such an event was left behind with waste strewn about, albeit over a fairly small area. Doubtless youngsters were watching and being taught how to make tools themselves, and

inevitably careless fingers were being hit and cut (**colour plate 3**).

Anthropological research carried out over the years has also given us an indication of how hunter–fisher–gatherer cultures conduct themselves. Generally speaking, the uplands tend to have been used as seasonal hunting grounds. The main occupation sites are usually located in the lowlands, with satellite sites in coastal areas to make best use of marine resources such as molluscs and fish at certain times of the year. Anthropologists suggest that the groups were often small, consisting of approximately twenty individuals who were mobile and exploited a variety of resources over the year.

Work by Simmons and Caseldine, among others, on a variety of sites has generated pollen diagrams which clearly illustrate how the vegetation of the moor has changed through time. At the onset of the Mesolithic, Dartmoor appears to have been largely open heath with small pockets of willows and birches in sheltered sites. As the climate improved after the last Ice Age, increasing quantities of deciduous trees including hazel, oak and elm appear in the pollen record and by 7000 BC most of Dartmoor was wooded. This deciduous woodland remained largely undisturbed until about 5000 BC when a sudden entry of bracken, grasses and weeds combined with a proportional decrease in tree pollen indicates substantial deforestation at the tree line. The most likely cause of this deforestation is fire, an argument supported by the recovery of charcoal from Black Ridge Brook and Pinswell. Such changes are recorded elsewhere in Britain and are thought to be the result of deliberately set forest fires. After fires, the regeneration of grazing plants made an area more attractive to ungulates such as red deer, and the removal of the tree cover meant that they could be more easily hunted. Here we seem to be seeing the first evidence of deliberate manipulation of the environment. Simmons has suggested that the build-up of deep blanket-peat deposits started immediately after the clearance of the woodland. It is, therefore, possible to equate the areas of present-day deep peat with those areas deforested during the Mesolithic (**11**).

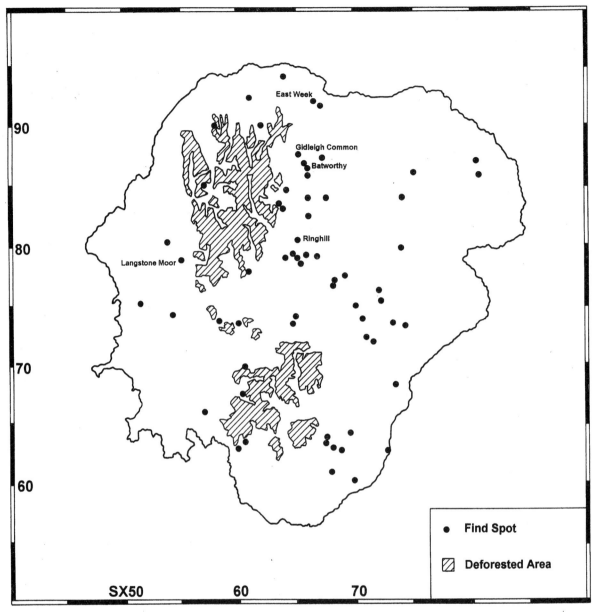

11 *The distribution of mesolithic flint tools tells only part of the story. None has yet been recovered from the areas of deep peat which are known to have been extensively exploited at this time. The flint distribution in part is a direct result of modern ploughing which has brought the tools to the surface. (Source: Devon SMR.)*

Neolithic (c. 4500–2300 BC)

The first seeds that were planted and observed by our ancestors in the latter part of the Mesolithic had a dramatic effect. Not only did these seeds bear fruit in the literal sense, but metaphorically they grew in the minds of their human observers in such a way as to transform all elements of human existence in a most fundamental way. With the transition from hunting and foraging in small groups to the domestication of animal and plant species – and their subsequent husbandry – came total reorganization of cultural practices, settlements, innovation and the evolution of industrialization, planning, technical improvements, a more sedentary and subsequently larger population, ceramics, the evolution of increasingly complex social hierarchies and the development of ritual or religious architecture. For these reasons the period known somewhat dryly as the 'Neolithic' should never be underestimated.

The seeds of innovation – development, observation and experimentation – germinated and grew, thus enabling humankind to become what it is today. The arguments which revolve around the cause of this complex and complete alteration on the perspective of human existence are well documented and erudite. For this reason there is insufficient space to do them justice here. However, as the archaeology of Dartmoor reveals, such changes did occur, and this evidence forms the basis of the following investigation.

The transition from hunter-gatherer to farmer was a slow one and evidence available from Britain as a whole suggests that in the early centuries of the Neolithic, farming played only a very small, though increasing, role in the economy.

Environmental evidence from the peat bogs is most informative on Dartmoor and indicates that the deciduous woodlands were being cleared and replaced with cultivated areas in which crops were grown. Many of these clearances appear to have been used only for a very short time, as there is evidence that regeneration of the forest followed. It seems most plausible that Neolithic agricultural activity was limited to sporadic clearance of small areas within the woodland using fire to remove trees and fertilize the ground which was to be cultivated. Then followed a short period of cultivation, during which the quality of the soil declined until a point was reached at which it was more productive to clear another area nearby. The original area was left uncultivated and within a short time trees generally recolonized it. For this slash-and-burn form of shifting agriculture to succeed, there must have been plenty of available land. There would have been no need to define ownership of particular clearings by building boundaries, and in any case the cultivated areas were probably abandoned after such a short period that there was very little point in spending time building walls which would soon be abandoned. In some cases the clearings may have needed protection from foraging animals, but portable wattle hurdles would have been easier to erect and probably more effective than stone walls. Archaeologically, this form of shifting agriculture has generally left no traces which existing fieldwork techniques can detect.

In some locations, however, circumstances may have led to traces of the cultivation areas being fossilized. In particularly stony areas, surface stones may have been removed and piled along the edges of the clearing producing a spread of rubble defining at least part of the original area. Well-preserved examples have recently come to light on Bodmin Moor near Stowes Pound and on Langstone Downs, where careful fieldwork by Hooley has indicated that spreads of rubble surrounding clearly defined stone-free areas are earlier than the associated Bronze Age fields (Dave Hooley, pers. comm.). On Dartmoor similar areas of cleared ground surrounded by low, ill-defined rubble banks have been found on the lower east-facing slopes of Roos Tor and at Trowlesworthy within the vicinity of the stone rows. Areas of Neolithic cultivation will have been destroyed by later agricultural activity, but despite this, examples of this earliest phase of farming surely remain to be identified (**colour plate 4**).

We should not underestimate the scale of observation, innovation and technical achievement which these practices represent. The production of hurdles and clearance of stone to facilitate the improvement of yields may seem obvious to us now, but these achievements were only made by observation, experimentation and calculation. Imagine, for example, that you had never seen a fence, and such a concept was alien to you. Would you have been able to design and invent such a structure, and all the tools it took to make it? Would you have thought to experiment with different materials, to learn from and develop your designs? These questions begin to suggest the complexity and enormity of changes to human concepts and ingenuity.

Despite the fact that the population was known to have increased and become more sedentary

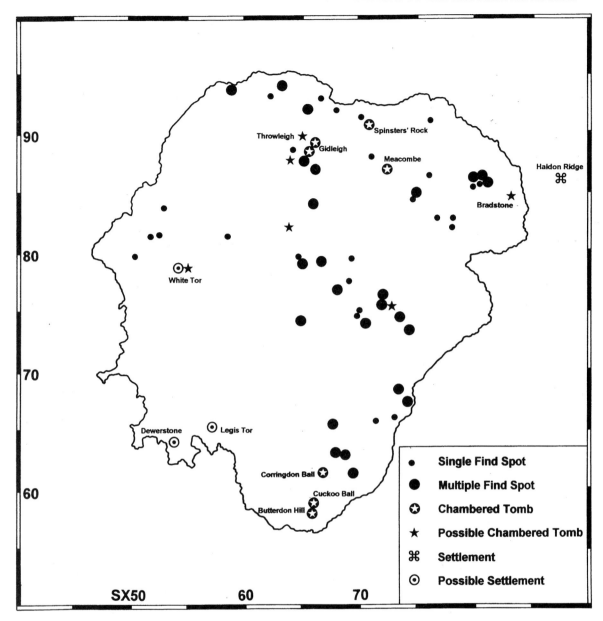

12 *The distribution of Neolithic flint tools probably owes more to the location of modern ploughing than anything else. It does however confirm that there was considerable activity in the area during this period. (Source: Devon SMR.)*

during this period, archaeologically there would appear to be a dearth of specifically Neolithic dwellings or settlements. Undoubtedly they did exist, but in an age before 'environmental issues' our ancestors appear to have built houses which were, to quote the modern vernacular,

'biodegradable'. As a result, evidence for settlements tends to come via the non-biodegradable detritus that was left behind. At Legis Tor some pottery is thought to be of Neolithic date and may indicate occupation during this period. However, doubt has been expressed regarding its identification. Despite this, the possibility still exists that, given the poor dating of the vast majority of round houses, some at least may have Neolithic origins. More conclusive evidence would seem to come from discrete scatters of flint (**12**).

Interestingly, one of the densest concentrations of Neolithic flint implements comes from the same fields at Batworthy where significant numbers of Mesolithic finds were made. This appears to be no coincidence as at least twelve sites have been found where both Mesolithic and Neolithic artefacts have been recovered together during fieldwalking. In itself this evidence does not prove continuity, but it does perhaps at least point to similar criteria being used in the selection of habitation sites.

Flint scatters generally indicate the location of those settlements which have been obliterated probably by the ploughing which has uncovered them. Further flint scatters are likely to come to light in the future, but because much of Dartmoor is not currently ploughed, many settlements levelled by post-Neolithic agricultural activity and consequently only detectable from flint and pottery scatters, are likely to remain hidden for some time. The best-preserved Neolithic settlements are likely to survive on the upper moorland beyond the reaches of Bronze Age cultivation, although despite intensive field survey none has yet been found. The most plausible explanation for this situation is that they were constructed using readily available timber cut down and fashioned to shape using the stone axes found at numerous locations. The building of wooden houses is a tradition which we know, from several excavated sites, to have continued into later periods. The archaeologist is thus faced with the problem of trying to understand a landscape in which we know there to have been considerable activity but, because most of the structures were probably constructed from biodegradable materials, there are no readily identifiable earthwork remains.

In order to form a parallel picture of the type of dwelling which was likely to have existed, it is necessary to examine a site which lies only a short distance outside the National Park boundary. A Neolithic structure on Haldon Ridge was excavated by Willock between 1934 and 1937. A rectangular timber framed building measuring 7m (23ft) long and 3.5m (11ft 6in) wide was unearthed. The walls consisted of daub resting on a stone and clay foundation and the gabled roof was supported on a ridge pole. Within the interior a basin-shaped cooking pit containing pottery and bone was found, together with a possible internal partition and two clay floors separated by a thin layer of sand. A large quantity of artefacts was also recovered during the excavation. These included a large number of flint tools, cores and flakes indicative of flintworking, and the butt of an unpolished dolerite axe.

It is at this point that one appreciates how fortunate we are that later generations turned to durable stone for building purposes and, in the process, left behind a remarkable settlement pattern for which the moor is justifiably well-known.

Two settlement sites on Dartmoor have been recognized as being potentially Neolithic in date, although it is important to emphasize that because they survive as visible monuments, they are probably atypical of most settlement sites of the period. These sites are situated on the hilltops at White Tor and Dewerstone and are morphologically similar to other sites in the south-west of England which have evidence of Neolithic settlement (**13**).

13 *The hilltop enclosure at White Tor lies in the centre of this photograph. The other enclosure attached to boundary banks (reaves) is considered to be of Bronze Age date. (BAD 14, Cambridge University Collection of Air Photographs: copyright reserved.)*

14 *The chamber of the tomb at Spinsters' Rock would have originally been partly covered by a long mound of stones. (Author.)*

The site at White Tor (also known as Whittor) was excavated by the Dartmoor Exploration Committee in 1898–9, though unfortunately only a few undatable flints were recovered. However, visible within the interior of the enclosure are a number of distinctive rectangular areas from which surface stone has been cleared. These may represent the sites of buildings similar to those found and excavated at Helman Tor and Carn Brea in Cornwall. Additional indirect support for the Neolithic date is perhaps provided by the proximity of a possible small chambered tomb. Evidence for settlements within relatively strongly defended sites seems to suggest pressures on the available resources. Further evidence to support the idea that there was indeed competition for land is provided by the appearance of strategically positioned substantial monuments such as chambered tombs and stone rows (**14**). Considerable effort was expended on building these often impressive monuments, and although the spiritual significance may have been the prime motivation to their builders, they may also have acted as territorial markers and status symbols.

The building of these large monuments indicates the considerable advances in technological and cultural change, as well as a departure from a purely subsistence existence and provides the first evidence of communal activity implying a greater level of social organization. For the first time, people considered it important to engage in communal activities that involved their working together to change the landscape deliberately for reasons other than simple survival. This change must have been associated with significant social and cultural developments which we can only surmise, since archaeological methods cannot indicate mental and spiritual attitudes directly. Such changes indicate a level of sophistication which appears to be absent from earlier cultures. Although details of their culture and social framework will never be known for certain, it is possible to gain an insight by examining their ritual monuments. Large chambered tombs represent significant physical effort and social organization. They were of specific importance in the disposal of the dead (**15**). The acid soils of the moor means that the bones deposited within these structures have not survived, but it is known from other areas of the country that often only certain selected bones were permanently placed in these tombs. It is also known that they were communal vaults designed for successive burials and that they probably formed a focus for the community; ethnographic studies throughout the world may lead us to imagine a culture with a strong emphasis upon the 'ancestors'. We are, then, perhaps looking at a people with a strong cultural sense of their past, present and future – a people with a strong sense of identity and allegiance. The size of the various communities cannot be established from the archaeological evidence, but the relatively small number and distribution of these robust monuments may reflect a few territories focused on the fringes of present-day moorland. However, despite the undisputed physical effort, social organization and planning which produced these monuments,

we cannot assume the complete cessation of a nomadic lifestyle. Territorial elements which these monuments appear to represent were becoming more important as populations grew and pressure for available land intensified. It would not have been unusual for selected parts of dead group members (especially skulls and long bones) to have been brought over considerable distances to their final resting places. We should not assume that permanent settlements would automatically be located in the immediate vicinity of such sepulchres. Also of note is the comparison between time expended on building settlements for the living, against those for the

15 *Chambered tombs are also known as long cairns and the chamber itself is often called a cromlech. Mounds similar to those found at these four sites would have originally formed part of the Spinsters' Rock chamber. (After Butler 1993, Fletcher et al. 1974a and Turner 1980.)*

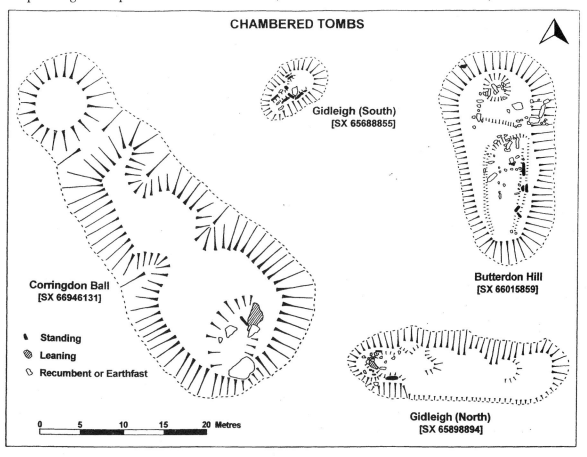

CHAMBERED TOMBS

Gidleigh (South)
[SX 65688855]

Butterdon Hill
[SX 66015859]

Corringdon Ball
[SX 66946131]

Standing
Leaning
Recumbent or Earthfast

0   5   10   15   20 Metres

Gidleigh (North)
[SX 65898894]

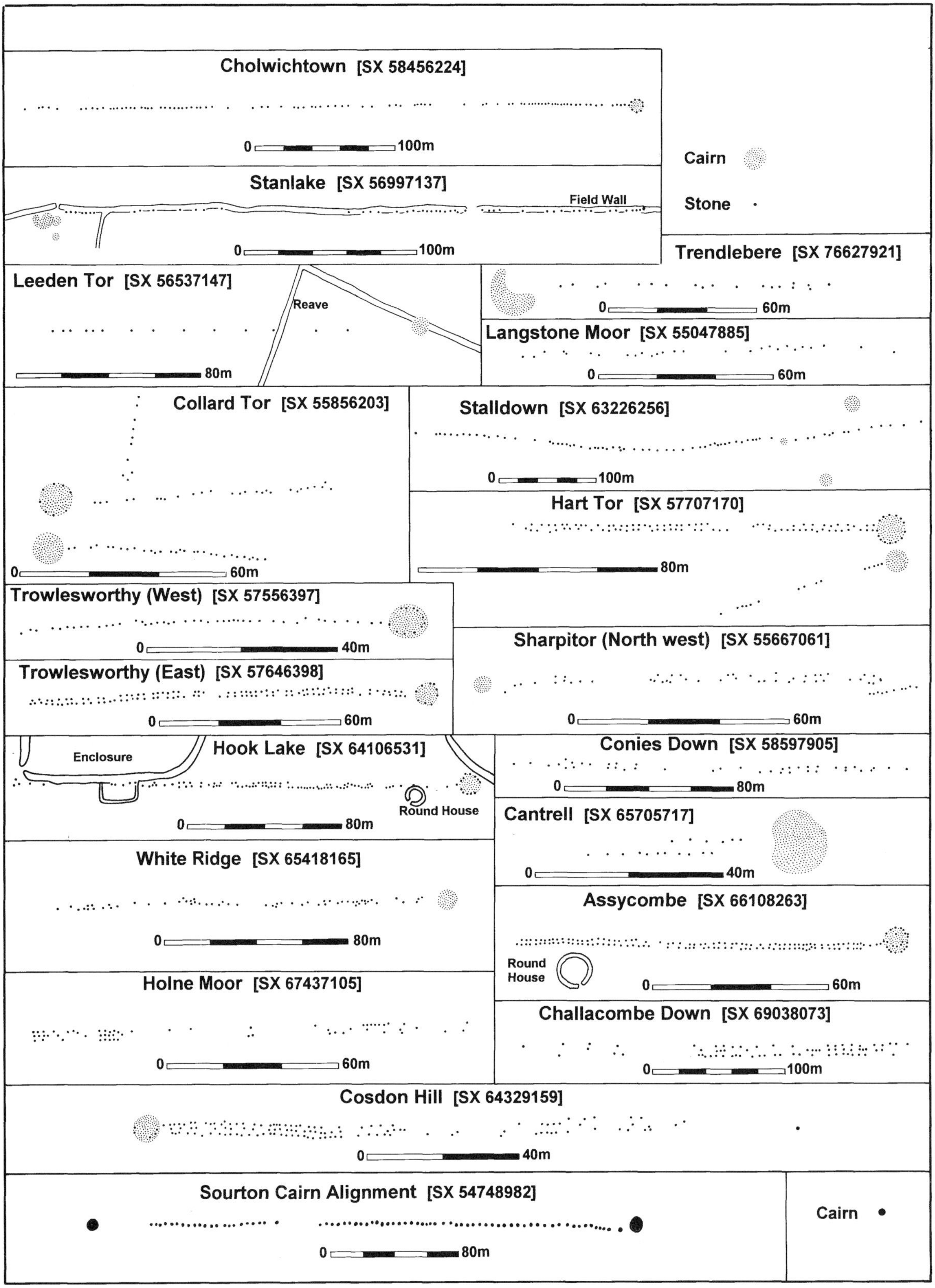

Cholwichtown [SX 58456224]

0 ⊢———⊣ 100m

Cairn

Stone ·

Stanlake [SX 56997137]

Field Wall

0 ⊢———⊣ 100m

Trendlebere [SX 76627921]

Leeden Tor [SX 56537147]

Reave

0 ⊢———⊣ 60m

0 ⊢———⊣ 80m

Langstone Moor [SX 55047885]

0 ⊢———⊣ 60m

Collard Tor [SX 55856203]

Stalldown [SX 63226256]

0 ⊢———⊣ 100m

0 ⊢———⊣ 60m

Hart Tor [SX 57707170]

0 ⊢———⊣ 80m

Trowlesworthy (West) [SX 57556397]

0 ⊢———⊣ 40m

Sharpitor (North west) [SX 55667061]

Trowlesworthy (East) [SX 57646398]

0 ⊢———⊣ 60m

0 ⊢———⊣ 60m

Enclosure **Hook Lake** [SX 64106531]

Round House

0 ⊢———⊣ 80m

Conies Down [SX 58597905]

0 ⊢———⊣ 80m

Cantrell [SX 65705717]

0 ⊢———⊣ 40m

White Ridge [SX 65418165]

0 ⊢———⊣ 80m

Assycombe [SX 66108263]

Round House

0 ⊢———⊣ 60m

Holne Moor [SX 67437105]

0 ⊢———⊣ 60m

Challacombe Down [SX 69038073]

0 ⊢———⊣ 100m

Cosdon Hill [SX 64329159]

0 ⊢———⊣ 40m

Sourton Cairn Alignment [SX 54748982]

0 ⊢———⊣ 80m

Cairn ·

32

16 The stone rows illustrated opposite are among the shorter examples. Most are associated with at least one funerary cairn. As can be clearly seen the length, ground plan and complexity varies considerably. (After Butler and OS Antiquity Cards.)

dead – in much the same sense as we compare the fine medieval churches and the housing of those times! Did the Neolithic people have a developed sense of 'religion' and continuity, or did they just believe that you were a long time dead? Certainly burial seems to have become an important rite of passage.

Other types of ritual monuments, some of which may have been built towards the end of this period, are the stone rows and perhaps some round cairns (**16**). Dating of the origin of these structures is presently uncertain although, particularly with the stone rows, it is clear that a number are earlier than some Bronze Age settlements, and for this reason they are considered here. At Hook Lake, for example, a Bronze Age enclosure and round house were constructed against an earlier and presumably disused double stone row while at Hurston Ridge another row was partially included within a similar enclosed settlement. At neither site were the stones forming the row removed for building purposes and this suggests that although no longer used, these structures still engendered sufficient respect to ensure their continued survival. Stone rows are among the most enigmatic of the prehistoric ritual monuments. At least seventy examples are known to survive and it is likely that there were once many more, particularly given their location on the fringes of current moorland (**17**). The rows include one or more lines of upright stones set at intervals and their lengths vary considerably from only a few metres to 3.32 kilometres (2.06 miles). Many of the rows are directly associated with round cairns, some of which are surrounded by a ring of prominent upright stone slabs (**18**). It is, however, not known whether these cairns were built at the same time as the rows or whether they were added at a later date and so represent another cultural response to

these sites. In addition to cairns placed close to the row there are many instances of other cairns lying within close proximity, and at some sites enclosures which may have also had some sort of ritual function have been noted (**19**). At Hingston Hill a circular enclosure lies within 110m (360ft) of a particularly visually impressive row, while at Corringdon Ball a rectangular enclosure survives within the vicinity of four separate rows.

Only the row at Cholwichtown has been excavated, and despite the examination of its entire length and the immediate surroundings, the only additional features identified were the sockets from which thirty-eight stones had been removed. Pollen analysis, however, indicates that the row had been constructed within an oak-forest clearing in which cereals had been grown. The only other site where palaeo-environmental work has been carried out is at the row on Holne Moor, where analysis of phosphates within the soil hinted at the site of a burial.

The most comprehensive analysis of stone rows is that by Emmett, who examined and compared the many characteristics of these monuments including their length, row spacing, stone spacing, stone size, row orientation, siting, distribution and environment. The results of this analysis were useful in suggesting that some rows were built over a period of time; none could have been utilized for astronomical purposes; and most were probably erected within previously cultivated forest clearances. The debunking of the astronomical theory is based on a number of criteria, but most significantly he argues convincingly that the irregularity of the individual rows and the considerable variety in their alignments means that as a group they pay little heed to celestial bodies. Sadly his work was unable to point to a function for these structures and thus until large-scale excavation of a site is attempted, much of our ignorance concerning this type of monument must remain. Most of the stone rows have been surveyed at least once and some several times. Interestingly each fresh survey has often produced slightly different results, with earlier stones not being found and on occasion large

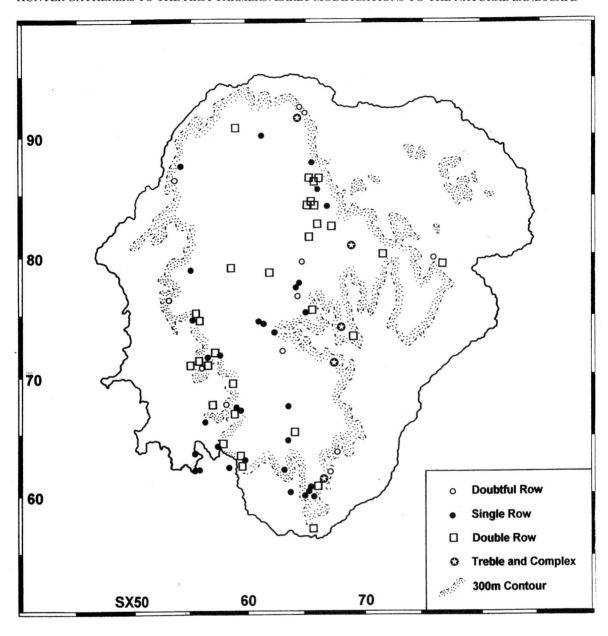

90

80

70

60

Doubtful Row

Single Row

Double Row

Treble and Complex

300m Contour

SX50   60   70

17 *Most of the stone rows lie close to the 300m contour which represents the approximate upper limit of historic cultivation. For this reason it is not possible to be sure whether the distribution is real and represents a preference by their builders for the type of location offered by this altitude or represents that part of the original distribution which survived later intensive agricultural activity. (After Emmett 1979 and Devon SMR.)*

18 *The Hingston Hill stone row survives remarkably well together with its terminal kerbed cairn. It is one of the most photogenic rows on Dartmoor. (Author.)*

19 *Stone rows together with cairns are found in close proximity to settlements. At Drizzlecombe, although the rows are set apart from the settlement, the cairn distribution extends into the areas between the enclosures. By contrast, at Shovel Down and Merrivale the ritual monument and settlement distributions are mutually exclusive, though in both cases, probable later prehistoric boundaries impinge on the ritual monument area. On Hingston Hill there is no associated settlement and on Hurston Ridge the enclosed settlement clearly postdates the row. (After Butler 1991b, 1994; Mercer 1986 and OS Antiquity Card.)*

numbers of fresh ones being recorded. Many of these differences can be explained in terms of the peat deposits, through which many of the rows protrude. In dry summers the peat shrinks and the result may be that fresh stones are uncovered, while in damp seasons these stones and ones that were previously visible may be engulfed by the swollen peat.

Archaeological answers regarding the function of these rows have proved elusive. There have been many interpretations from the apparently

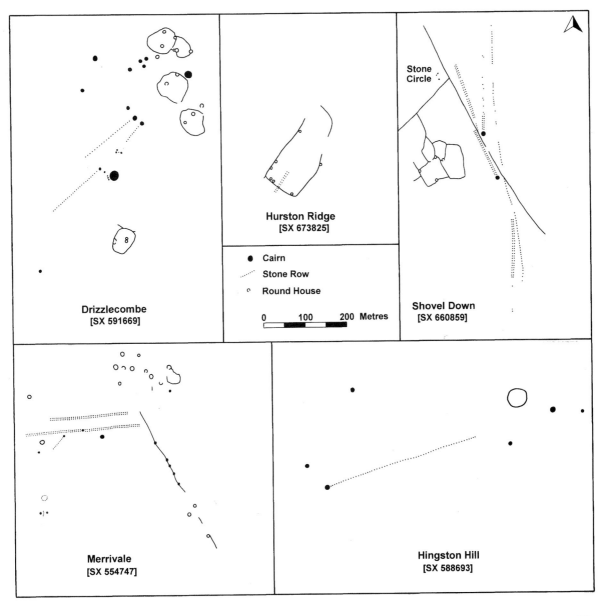

sensible to the downright incredible. Enigmatic they still remain, though science may one day put to rest our vivid imaginings and reduce flamboyant theories to cold facts. Within the wild moorland landscapes at present, however, our human imagination is left to fantasize and speculate. Any one of us may yet be proved right.

A site which may be related in some way to the stone rows is the cairn alignment on Sourton Common recently identified and surveyed by Turner. This includes a 344m (1,130ft) line of at least seventy-four small cairns lying between two larger mounds. At this site, cairns appear to have replaced the more common upright stones, but their function and purpose may have been identical.

A large number of small burial cairns are found closely associated with stone rows. These may also date to the Neolithic, although irrefutable evidence for this is lacking. Elsewhere in Britain much larger and often spectacular sepulchral barrows are known to have had Neolithic origins. By implication, therefore, some of the larger cairns on Dartmoor might also prove to be attributable to this period.

Although we would perhaps like to believe that life was less complicated in the Neolithic, the evidence we have suggests exactly the opposite. The building of defended sites, chambered tombs and the other ritual monuments all bear witness to a heightened level of social organization, planning and spiritual identity, possibly a sort of proto-patriotism. Evidence suggests the clearance of forests, cultivation of crops and probable continuation of earlier survival strategies. People were undoubtedly worrying about the same basic issues that are still troubling us in the twentieth century, and in this regard, the human condition is much as it ever was. However, the basic foundations for identifying land divisions and cultural identity had already been laid. In subsequent years these would be consolidated and technologically improved to produce the most dramatic landscape ever seen on Dartmoor.

3
The solid imprint of the Bronze Age: settlements, field-systems and cairns

It is to the Bronze Age (*c.* 2300–700 BC) that most of the surviving prehistoric archaeological structures are considered to belong. The landscape bears witness to the development of cultural and social change. Ritual stone rows continued to be used together with stone circles. Cairns for the dead punctuate the landscape, but now these contain individuals and not groups of people. Stone-built settlements and their associated fields appear across the moor. Most remarkable of all, from both a cultural and logistical viewpoint, is the emergence by the Middle Bronze Age (*c.* 1400–1000 BC) of several large and well-defined

20 *This round house lies just below the high water level within Fernworthy Reservoir and is generally only exposed during the summer months. The figure is standing just outside the doorway. (Chris Powell: copyright reserved.)*

'territories' denoted by a complex series of boundary banks called 'reaves'.

Settlements

Dartmoor contains a rich array of archaeological remains relating to the settlement of the area during the Bronze Age, with over 5000 stone-built round houses having been identified so far (**20**). Compared with earlier periods, the survival of so many structures together with their fields and enclosures means that it is possible to examine, for the first time, the character and nature of settlement. Impressive though the picture may seem, we should never lose sight of the fact that excavation has demonstrated that timber buildings and other structures continued to be erected and that therefore the evidence provided by the stone structures can only represent part of the overall picture.

A common feature of all settlements are the round houses which generally survive as stone and earth walls surrounding a circular or oval internal area (**21**). Round houses vary considerably in character and a typology based on the different construction methods and ground plans has been developed to highlight the similarities and differences between the individual buildings. Using this typology, a sample of 1500 houses has

been examined and the results are presented here (**Table 2**). Other characteristics of round houses include internal partitions and doorways. Preliminary fieldwork indicates that only just

21 *Simplified plans of some excavated round houses. The size, shape and character of round houses varies considerably. (After Fox 1954, 1957; Wainwright and Smith 1980; and Worth 1981.)*

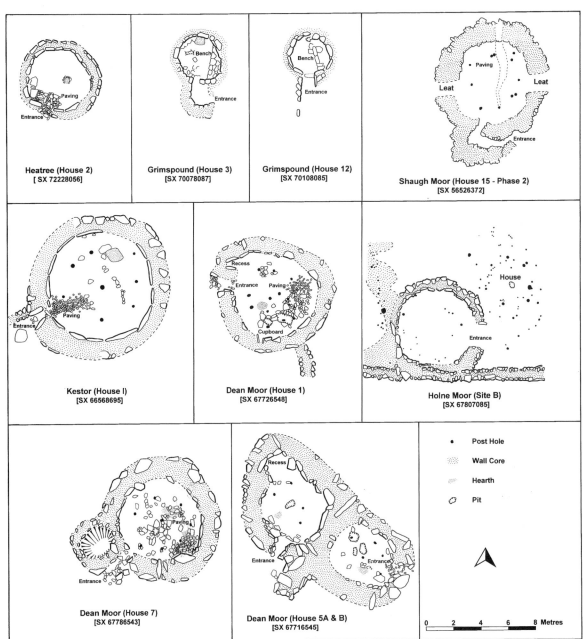

Heatree (House 2)
[SX 72228056]

Grimspound (House 3)
[SX 70078087]

Grimspound (House 12)
[SX 70108085]

Shaugh Moor (House 15 - Phase 2)
[SX 56526372]

Kestor (House I)
[SX 66568695]

Dean Moor (House 1)
[SX 67726548]

Holne Moor (Site B)
[SX 67807085]

Dean Moor (House 7)
[SX 67786543]

Dean Moor (House 5A & B)
[SX 67716545]

· Post Hole
Wall Core
Hearth
Pit

0 2 4 6 8 Metres

WALLING TYPE (%)

PLAN TYPE	Single upright stones	Double upright stones	Rubble bank	Coursed	Total (%)
Simple plan	22.54	15.40	35.36	11.83	85.13
Porch	0.73	0.79	0.59	0.40	2.51
Screen	0	0	0	0.07	0.07
Conjoined	3.64	1.59	4.16	1.19	10.58
With annex or forecourt	0.20	0.26	0.85	0.40	1.71
Total (%)	26.92	17.93	40.71	13.79	100

Table 2 *Characteristics of round houses. Simple plan houses with rubble walling are most common, although 10 per cent of all buildings are what we would now call semi-detached. The low percentage of houses with porches and screens may reflect difficulties in identifying these features in the field. (Author.)*

under 2 per cent of these houses have visible partitions while 43 per cent have clearly defined doorways. Some 43 per cent of the houses are connected to field or enclosure walls, although this figure clearly underestimates the original situation since some at least may have been attached to timber fences which no longer survive. The internal diameters of the houses vary considerably – from as little as 1.2m to 10.7m (3ft 11in to 35ft 1in) with the average being 4.44m (14ft 7in). These buildings must have served a variety of functions for not all of them were dwellings; the smaller ones in particular may have been storage buildings. The height of the surrounding walls average 0.58m (1ft 11in) but some are as low as 0.1m (4in), others as high as 1.7m (5ft 7in), although the higher walls may have been rebuilt at a later date. The orientation of entrances may give us clues concerning the character of settlement. At some settlements the orientation of the doorways appears haphazard, while at others all or most of the doorways appear to have a southerly or easterly aspect in order to avoid the prevailing bitter north-west winds. Fleming has suggested that these differences may indicate largely seasonal occupation of those sites with a varying doorway orientation and permanent occupation of those with doors facing away from the prevailing winter winds. If this is the case it would appear that the upland was occupied by a large population throughout the year as most settlements appear to have had their entrances sited to take account of the winter winds. Exceptions to this include settlements at Roos Tor, White Tor and Cosdon Hill (W) where a significant proportion of the house entrances appear to face unfavourable aspects. Future work may be able to confirm the validity of this approach and perhaps provide further information on the character of settlement. Door orientation may alternatively be a result of social interaction. A good example would be a typical modern campsite. Some people deliberately face away from others to preserve their privacy. Others locate the doorway to enable themselves to both 'see' and be 'seen' by their fellows and so to instigate social interaction. Some groups pitch their tents in a circle, with their doors facing onto the central space (the communal area). This tends to indicate social interaction but only within the group. Of course, there are those who pitch their doorways sensibly away from prevailing winds, to take in a fine view, or those who simply pitch a tent! The whole of human experience may be observed at a campsite.

Finally, many of the houses were re-used during the prehistoric and the historic period (see **7**) and although this activity does not always leave clear signs, there is evidence at over 3 per cent of the round houses of either rebuilding or adaptation.

Antiquarian and archaeological excavations have provided the evidence to support the assumption that most of the round-house settlements belong to the middle part of the Bronze Age, though these same excavations have indicated that some houses at least were re-occupied during the Iron Age. Between 1894 and 1905 the Dartmoor Exploration Committee excavated some 200 houses within 22 settlements. This work revealed considerable differences between individual houses and settlements. Their reports, although brief, taken together provide a useful source of information concerning the character of round houses.

The excavations carried out by the Exploration Committee together with others by later archaeologists, have provided a wealth of information concerning the structure and character of houses. In general terms, construction of the houses began with the clearance of overlying turf and topsoil. The internal floor was usually made up of the decomposed gravelly granite known as 'growan'. Where huts were built into the hillside, more intricate construction was needed to keep them level inside. At House 4, Legis Tor, for example, the downslope side was backfilled with stone rubble and paved. All houses have paved thresholds and many have steps down into them. Some have the luxury of a paved yard outside, but no excavated huts have complete internal stone-flooring. It is assumed that the roofs of the huts were conical and thatched with turves or heather. The roof was either supported by a circular collar around the walls or, as at Shapley Common (House 1) and Langstone Moor (House 10), with a central pole, the evidence for which was found in excavation.

Of course, to us as individuals, houses are often of particular interest. On a basic level we begin to see how our ancestors lived out their daily lives. Archaeology, in this sense, is very personal, because it deals directly with the homes and belongings of individuals to whom we may feel we can relate. Understandably, within the houses, hearths were especially important as a focal point. These were often constructed from slabs of granite, just higher than the surrounding floor and frequently fire-cracked. Occasionally we find a stone surround or, more often, merely a charcoal patch with no stones at all. Only one house (Rider's Rings, House 2) could be said to

contain a 'fireplace'. This consisted of a slab or stone set on edge and propped up at an angle, with a shallow pit beneath. The position of the hearth varies considerably, being either central or set to one side.

Cooking facilities are another important component, and there are two distinct types. The first is a 'cooking hole', a small pit sunk into the floor and occasionally lined with stone, such as at House 12 at Hart Tor. These pits, which were used for baking, vary in size and shape. Stones (pot-boilers) were heated in the fire and placed into the hole with the food (perhaps a small joint of meat), more stones were used to fill the remaining space and the whole covered with ashes. The second type is the cooking-pot hole. This contained a rough earthenware pot, not designed to be removed. It too was set into the floor. It was partly filled with water, then stones heated in the nearby fire (the pot-boilers) were added to boil the water or soup. Two perfect examples have been found, one at Legis Tor, House 7, and the other at Raddick, House 5. The pots had hemispherical bases and the Legis Tor example had been repaired without being removed. Of course, placing hot stones into cold water would often shatter the pot-boilers. Bronze Age cuisine must have frequently contained many hard lumps!

Some houses contain a raised 'bench' around the walls. These are rarely higher than 0.2m (8in) and are either on the right-hand side of the entrance or directly opposite the door. There are examples of both types at Grimspound and they are thought to represent the seating and sleeping areas of the huts.

Other evidence for daily life within a Dartmoor Bronze Age house comes from the surviving artefacts. Charcoal is the most common, most of it being derived from peat, twigs and small logs of oak, alder, furze and willow. Cooking stones or pot-boilers are also common finds and these are frequently fire-cracked. Pottery was chiefly used for cooking-vessels and containers. The storage vessels are often decorated with incised patterns, thumbnails, imprints, dots, lines and chevrons. The pottery itself is handmade, thick, coarse and underbaked. Worked flints have also been found in large quantities and include scrapers and occasional arrowheads. More unusual discoveries include soft slickstones which may have been used to rub down and soften skins and coarse fabrics, a possible spindle whorl for spinning wool, red ochre which may have been used as a dye, and a drill made from a quartz crystal. Sadly no bronze artefacts have survived within the huts, though their use is inferred from the recovery of whetstones on which blades would have been sharpened.

Together, this variety of artefactual evidence bears testimony to the large number of different agricultural pursuits and related activities practised by the people living on the moor during the Bronze Age.

The settlements have been examined using a diverse array of techniques. Many have been excavated, most have been surveyed and these have been the subject of individual and collective interpretation. The earliest work recognized a distinct dichotomy in settlement types. In the north-eastern part of the moor, these generally included small numbers of houses scattered within field-systems. Elsewhere, however, larger numbers of dwellings were clustered together either within, or associated with, enclosures and a few fields. The explanation for this phenomenon was thought to lie with climatic differences, the settlements on the eastern side being seen as lying within an area of lower rainfall and so better suited to arable cultivation, while those elsewhere were concerned largely with animal husbandry on soils which were too wet to stand prolonged cultivation. This interpretation remains popular but does not explain what is in reality a much more complex situation. Detailed examination of settlement types is made easier using a typology. One developed by Hamond identified nine different types of settlement. Further refinement of this typology is necessary to take into account complex enclosure patterns visible at many sites.

There is no such thing as 'the typical Bronze Age settlement', and once you start to examine the detail, it becomes clear that, in much the same way as today's settlement pattern is extremely varied, so is that of the Bronze Age.

Settlements survive in a variety of sizes and forms and are associated with different contemporary features. At least 900 distinct prehistoric settlements have been recognized on Dartmoor (**22**). The map illustrates the nature of this distribution and emphasizes the dense character of the occupation during this period. In the southern part of the moor, groups of settlements lying within the narrow river valleys can be clearly distinguished. Elsewhere the reasons for spatial organization are less clear. The two relatively blank areas in the centre of the moor lie in areas where deep peat accumulation may have buried most surviving settlements, although it has been argued that these relatively inhospitable areas probably never carried a large population. The relatively sparse distribution within the north-eastern part of the National Park is the result of later agricultural re-use of this area. For comparative and analytical purposes the settlements have been divided into three main types. The first includes round houses not associated with enclosures; second are settlements associated with enclosures; and third are the settlements lying within fields.

In considering these settlement types it is often difficult using archaeological evidence alone to define precisely the extent of a settlement and its hinterland. This situation is further complicated in certain areas where groups of houses, enclosures and fields extend for a considerable distance, with little or no gap between the components of the settlement. A modern analogy would be those cities which, in their expansion, have absorbed previously separate nineteenth-century villages. However, in the case of the Bronze Age settlement, it is not known whether the final form was produced by infilling or by gradual development outwards from a central point. Some Dartmoor workers have defined these areas of dense concentrations as settlement complexes. At least twenty-three such complexes have been identified to date. One example is Littaford Tor where a total of fourteen enclosures, eighty round houses

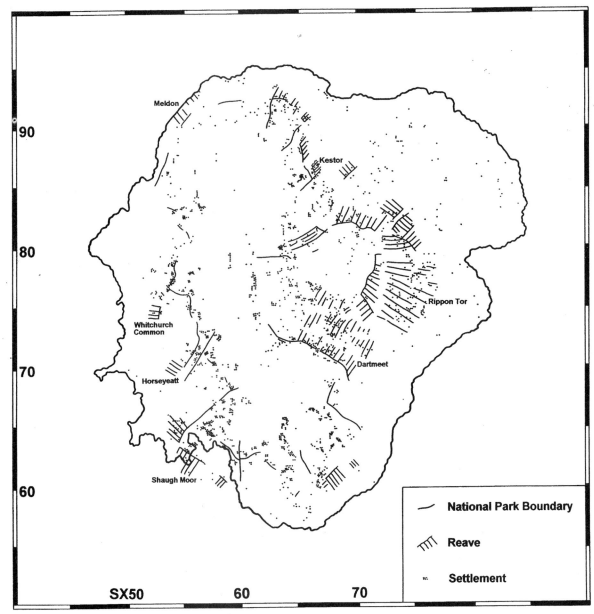

22 *The density of settlement combined with the vast scale of the reave systems can be easily appreciated. The band of settlement down the western side of the moor represents a tide line with the settlements to the west having been largely destroyed by later agricultural activity whilst the ground to the east was too inhospitable and was never occupied. In the south of the moor, three separate linear clusters of settlements represent those within the river valleys of the Plym, Erme and Avon. (After Fleming 1988 and Devon SMR.)*

and a fragmentary field-system lie scattered for 1.4km (0.8 miles) along a west-facing slope. Another is Small Brook situated within the valley of the River Taw (**23**) where the settlement complex comprises nine clusters of houses, amounting to a total of 121 buildings. Two of these clusters differ from the others in that there is no complete surviving enclosure boundary, although the layout of the buildings suggests that many of them may once have been connected by timber palisades. No field-system or even garden plots are visible within the vicinity of the complex and without any other evidence to the contrary it would appear likely that the inhabitants of this particular settlement were not involved in cultivation.

By contrast the farmers at the larger settlement complex at Watern Oke (see **23**) probably grew

23 *The settlement complexes at Small Brook and Watern Oke are different in character. One contains a number of separate enclosures, while the other includes houses with associated garden plots. Both, however, contain at least one cluster of seemingly unenclosed houses. (After Anderson 1906, Butler 1991b and Author.)*

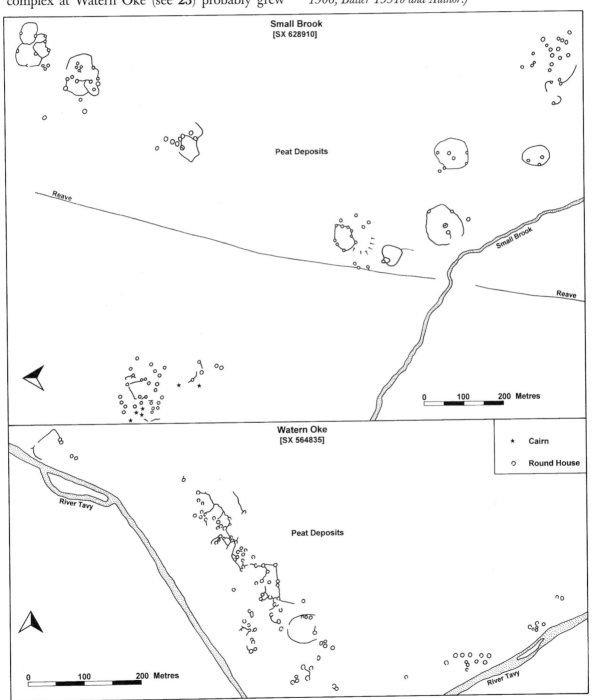

some crops in the small garden plots formed by low rubble walls running between many of their houses. Again there is no trace of a more extensive field-system, though this may of course lie beneath the nearby deep peat deposits. This settlement complex contains at least ninety-five round houses, many of which were excavated by the Dartmoor Exploration Committee in 1905. This work revealed that most contained occupation debris including cooking stones, flints and worked stones. In nearly half of the buildings hearths were found. However, information concerning the character of the economy at the settlement was not discovered. The settlement complex at Riddon Ridge survives together with an extensive irregular aggregate field-system. Nine others including the ones at Vag Hill (see **4**), Holne Moor (see **76**) and Corringdon Ball lie either wholly or partly within coaxial field-systems which are groups of fields arranged on a single prevailing axis, subdivided by transverse boundaries and demarcated by a terminal reave at either end. It would appear that settlement complexes are found associated with a variety of field-system types and enclosures, and as a settlement form they do not at present appear to be the result of any specific form of economic activity.

Most of the complexes have been altered to some extent by later activity, though the examples at Small Brook and west of Three Barrows appear to survive in their original form.

Settlements without enclosures or field-systems

The simplest form of settlement includes an isolated round house with no associated enclosure or fields. At least ninety-nine examples of this type of settlement are known, although no doubt many others await discovery. Some of these settlements may have been associated with upland seasonal grazing, and other examples may represent early phases of colonization which, for various reasons, did not develop any further. Logically, therefore, some of the houses within the larger and more complex settlements were probably once of this type. These houses may,

therefore, be particularly important for the information which they might provide concerning seasonal grazing practices (transhumance) and Early Bronze Age (c. 2300–1400 BC) colonization of the moor. Only one round house belonging to this type of settlement has been excavated, and unfortunately the example chosen at Western Red Lake by the Dartmoor Exploration Committee had been re-used as a shelter during the post-medieval period. The results of the work were therefore disappointing and shed no light on its date or function.

Another type of settlement includes clusters of freestanding houses associated with no visible walls or enclosures (**24**). Originally some of the houses within this type of settlement may have been connected to each other by palisades of timber similar to those found by Fleming at Site B on Holne Moor. Alternatively, in some cases, slightly built, low walls may have disappeared, being submerged by subsequent peat accumulation. This said, it is important to consider that since over 100 clusters of apparently freestanding houses are known, some at least were probably always unenclosed. To confirm this contention we turn to Shaugh Moor Site No. 15, where excavation demonstrated that the settlement was originally unenclosed and the visible boundary wall was added at a later date (see **9**). Further evidence comes from more than ninety other sites including Blatchford Bottom, Broad Hole and Brockhill Ford West, where some of the houses are butted by the enclosure boundary walls, indicating clearly that these houses were built first and the wall added at a later date (**25**). Apparently clusters of freestanding houses were once more common before some were enclosed at a later date. The question is why were some of these clusters enclosed while others were not? Perhaps those without enclosures were abandoned before such practices became a feature of the Dartmoor landscape. It is, of course, equally possible that some remained in use and were not enclosed for other reasons. Some of these settlements may have been associated with the exploitation of nearby tin deposits; indeed, the close association

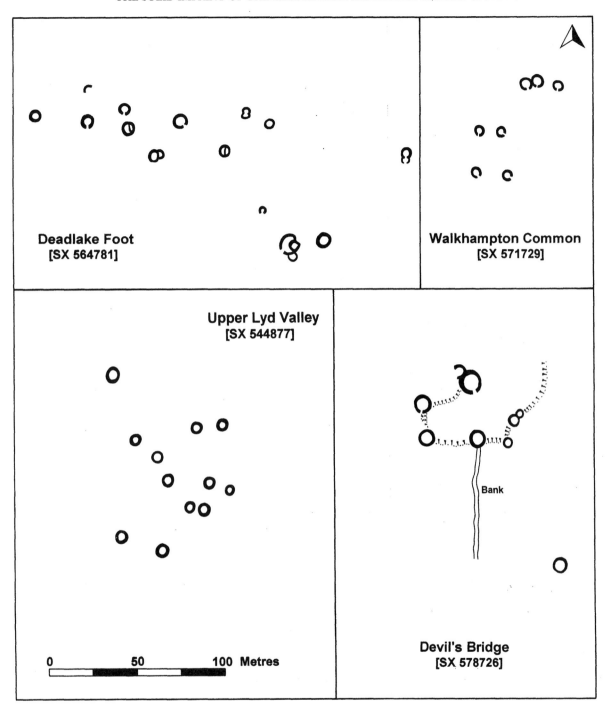

24 *The settlements at Deadlake Foot, Walkhampton Common and Upper Lyd Valley have no visible associated boundaries. The settlement at Devil's Bridge has always been previously recorded as being unenclosed, but recent fieldwork indicates that most of the houses here are connected by a slight scarp or lynchet indicating the position of a partly buried bank. Future fieldwork may reveal that unenclosed clusters of houses are indeed much rarer than current evidence would suggest. (Author.)*

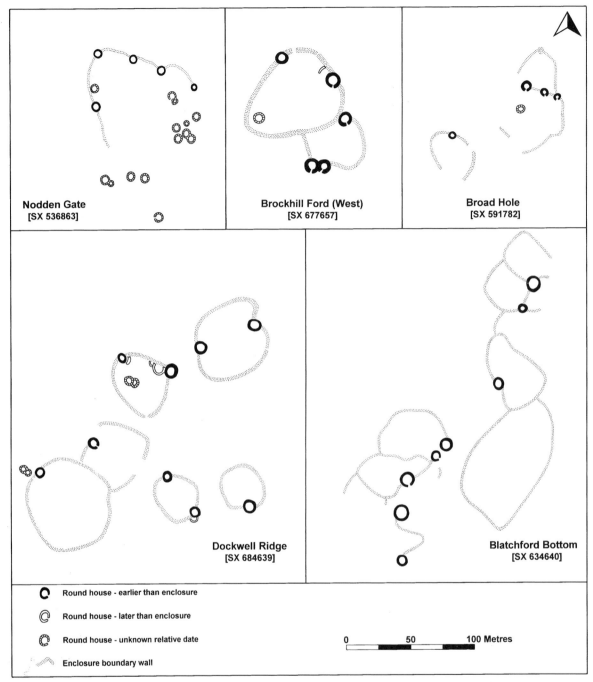

25 *Examples of settlements to which enclosures were added. Fieldwork indicates that many enclosure boundaries abut associated round houses confirming that the house was built before the enclosure. At some sites other houses abut the enclosures indicating that these examples were built after the enclosure. Together this evidence supports the idea that settlements were continually developing. (After Butler 1993 and Author.)*

of some to rich tin ground does seem to lend a modicum of support to this hypothesis. However, no examples of this type of settlement have been excavated and we must therefore merely speculate at this stage as to their date and function.

The third form of settlement includes a cluster of houses associated with garden plots, with some

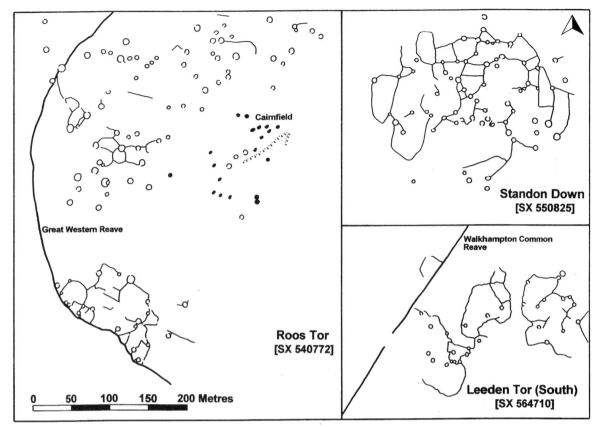

of the houses linked together by boundaries to form yards (**26**). There are at least forty known examples of this type of site. At Standon Down (a settlement excavated by the Dartmoor Exploration Committee in 1901), at least seventy houses sit in a tight group linked together by low rubble walls. The field evidence supports the hypothesis that this type of settlement supported a community which relied on both arable farming and animals for its survival. However, in all known examples, the relationship between the buildings and the connecting walls clearly indicates that the walls were added later. It appears that this type of settlement grew from clusters of unenclosed houses; at Roos Tor this process seems to have barely started with many of the huts remaining unattached, although perhaps most were connected by temporary hurdles which have left no surface trace. Some of the settlements contain a large number of buildings and only a relatively small area of associated garden plots and yards. The reasons for this apparent anomaly

26 *Some of the round houses within this type of settlement are connected to each other by low rubble walls forming garden plots and yards. Many houses, however, are not connected in this way and although there is no obvious explanation it may be a significant characteristic. (After Anderson 1902, RCHM[E] and OS Antiquity Card.)*

are unclear, particularly when one considers the extensive field-systems associated with many smaller settlements. The absence of large animal enclosures suggests that stock did not play a primary role within the settlements either. These observations have led some researchers to argue that at least some of these settlements may have been associated with tin exploitation. There is, however, no evidence to support this contention, and the absence of any tin-related artefacts from the extensive excavations at Watern Oke and Standon Hill would suggest that this explanation cannot be the answer. Many examples of this type of settlement lie on the edge of large areas where no other settlements have yet been found. It there-

27 *Rider's Rings, the large agglomerated enclosure in the foreground, is one of many settlements within the Avon valley. (RCHME: Crown Copyright SX 6764/4.)*

fore seems possible that at least some of them were exploiting the substantial tracts of higher moorland grazing and their animals were generally kept away from the settlement and catered for on the open moor, being brought down to the settlements only for slaughter. The associated garden plots would have been used perhaps to supply vegetables and cereals.

Enclosures

Settlements with associated enclosures are the most numerous recorded type on Dartmoor (**colour plate 5**). There are at least 488 of these and they are found in large numbers throughout the moor except in the north-east, where they are generally associated with extensive coaxial field-systems. The enclosures take two basic forms: simple and agglomerated, where two or more enclosures are attached to each other (**27**). Within this basic division, six main types of simple enclosure and a further six types of agglomerated

enclosure have been identified (**28** and **29**). A total of at least 437 settlements contain at least one simple enclosure, while agglomerated enclosures are found within 83 settlements. The shape and size of the enclosures vary considerably, although they are generally oval, sub-circular or circular. They survive as areas surrounded by a boundary wall, often comprising a rubble and earth bank, although on occasions a faced wall may be found. At some sites gaps in the wall may be identified as original entrances, while many are the result of later interference.

It is uncertain, in the absence of excavation, whether variations in the layout of settlements containing this type of enclosure are of real significance. The problem is exacerbated by our knowledge of other sites containing timber houses and enclosures where evidence does not survive above ground. For this reason it would be dangerous to read too much into what may in many instances be only partial evidence. The main benefit of examining the different types is to highlight possible differences in settlement layout which in turn may suggest variations in the farming practices adopted and the consequent economy and status of the settlement. Another equally plausible explanation is that the differences reflect variations in the way particular sites developed over time. Certainly, for example, the excavated evidence so far suggests that enclosures were added at some time after the erection of at least some of the houses. Those settlements with surviving enclosures were probably the subject of upgrading. **Table 3** lists examples of the different types of simple enclosed settlements and offers some possible interpretations.

Six different forms of settlements containing agglomerated enclosures have been identified.

The fundamental difference between these enclosures and those of the simple variety is that further enclosures were added to the original one. This suggests such sites developed over a period of time although obviously it is not possible to establish the duration without excavation. This type of enclosure is less common than the simple variety with only eighty-three known

28 *Settlements containing simple enclosures are amongst the most common, but they do vary considerably in form. (After Butler 1991b, 1992, 1993; Fox 1957; Mercer 1986; OS Antiquity Card; Wainwright and Smith 1980; and Author.)*

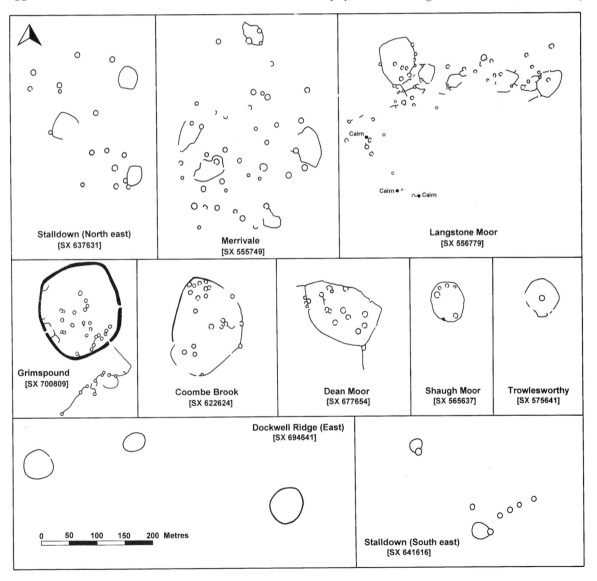

Stalldown (North east) [SX 637631]

Merrivale [SX 555749]

Langstone Moor [SX 556779]

Cairn

Cairn

Cairn

Grimspound [SX 700809]

Coombe Brook [SX 622624]

Dean Moor [SX 677654]

Shaugh Moor [SX 565637]

Trowlesworthy [SX 575641]

Dockwell Ridge (East) [SX 694641]

0   50   100   150   200 Metres

Stalldown (South east) [SX 641616]

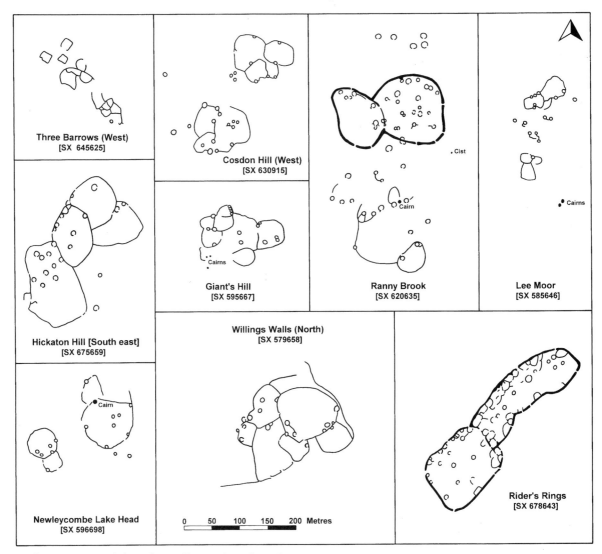

settlements containing them. Examples of settlements containing agglomerated enclosures are shown above (see **29**).

29 *Agglomerated enclosures demonstrate clearly the manner in which some settlements evolved. (After Butler, Mercer 1986 and Author.)*

Settlements lying within field-systems

The remaining major settlement type is that within field-systems. (The fields themselves are considered below.) These settlements generally include clusters of houses scattered within the field-system. In some cases it is clear that many houses had already been built before the field-systems were laid out as at Holne Moor where a field boundary diverts around House F, and within the northern part of Merrivale Newtake where most of the field boundaries clearly abut the earlier round houses.

Some 28 per cent of known settlements lie within or are attached to field-systems and of these 81 per cent are found with coaxial fields, 20 per cent with irregular aggregate fields and 1 per cent with cairn-fields. There does not appear to be any significant difference in the character of the houses found within the different types of field.

Land division and field-systems

Dramatic changes are witnessed during the Bronze Age where, for the first time, major territorial

Table 3 *Possible interpretations of settlements containing simple enclosures.*

TYPE EXAMPLES

	NGR(SX)	NAME	POSSIBLE INTERPRETATION OF FIELD EVIDENCE
A	637631 573651 559634 547645	Stalldown (NE)* Trowlesworthy Saddlesborough Lower Cadworthy	i. Animals corralled in nearby enclosure. ii. Stone houses abandoned and timber ones erected within a stone walled enclosure. iii. Timber houses within enclosure replaced by stone ones outside.
B	555749 556779 700809 677657 536863 684639	Merrivale* Langstone Moor* Grimspound* Brockhill Ford (W)* Nodden Gate* Dockwell Ridge*	i. Houses outside enclosure abandoned at time when enclosure erected. ii. Houses inside enclosure abandoned or re-used as animal shelters when enclosure built. iii. All houses continued in use after enclosure constructed, but may have served different functions.
C	622624 565637 591782 673825 635800 660663	Coombe Brook* Shaugh Moor Site 15* Broad Hole* Hurston Ridge* Broadun Huntingdon Warren	i. Enclosure constructed around existing settlement to exclude livestock. ii. Enclosure constructed around existing settlement to protect livestock. iii. Enclosure constructed around existing settlement to offer protection against marauders. iv. Enclosure constructed and the houses then added over a number of years.
D	575641	Trowlesworthy*	As C above
E	694641 584705 713803 658738	Dockwell Ridge (E)* Crazy Well* Berry Pound Huccaby Ring	i. Enclosure for holding livestock at some distance from the main settlement. ii. Enclosure around a settlement composed entirely of timber buildings. iii. Enclosure built around stone buildings which have since been robbed.
F	641616 624700	Stalldown (SE)* Fox Tor (N)	i. Enclosure definitely added to existing settlement. ii. Enclosure used either to hold or exclude livestock.

Type A: Houses adjacent to enclosure(s); B: Partially enclosed settlement;

C: Enclosure containing more than one house; D: Enclosure containing one house;

E: Enclosure(s) only; F: Enclosure(s) attached to house.

* Illustrated in this book

boundaries are introduced. This forms the basic framework upon which the individual communities hung their own particular agricultural field-systems. Therefore, we see two distinct levels of land subdivision: the territorial reaves, followed by three different approaches to agricultural activity indicated by coaxial field-systems, irregular aggregate field-systems and cairnfields. Agricultural activity was, however, not limited to these fields and the vast areas of unenclosed upland must have provided important grazing. Tangible archaeological remains of this activity are sparse, though the very size and number of settlements bordering the upland grazing areas supports the idea that this resource was maximized.

The scale of the territorial boundaries is huge. Important work by Fleming has shown that stone and earth boundaries known as reaves extend over vast tracts of moorland, and some serve to subdivide Dartmoor into several substantial territories. These survive most clearly in the southern part of the moor where a series of watershed and contour reaves divide the landscape into six distinct blocks, centred on the river valleys (see **22**). Each territory is then subdivided by further reaves, which on occasion appear to separate upland pasture from lowland grazing and arable. Once the territorial reaves were established, the various communities appear to have followed different approaches to agricultural practice.

Coaxial field-systems are groups of fields arranged on a single prevailing axis, subdivided by transverse boundaries and demarcated by a terminal reave at either end (**30** and see **4**, **76** and **77**). Fleming's work, particularly on the Dartmeet coaxial field-system, has shown clearly the level of information which can be derived from careful study of this type of landscape. The Dartmeet field-system covers about 3000 hectares and, though its eastern and western boundaries are not clearly defined, the core of the system is very well preserved and represented an excellent choice for study. A programme of detailed survey and limited excavation over a number of years was carried out. The size and regularity of the field-system at once points to it having been laid out in a single operation within a relatively open landscape devoid of any significant tree cover. The landscape upon which the field-system was imposed was, however, not empty and a number of earlier cairns, stone rows, settlements and field boundaries were already present. The attitude of the Bronze Age surveyors to these earlier structures does not appear to have been consistent with, for example, the stone rows at Yar Tor and Sherberton Common being ignored while the one on Holne Moor appears to have been deliberately excluded. The Dartmeet system appears, like

30 *This minuscule part of the Rippon Tor coaxial field-system lies on Horridge Common. The fields surrounding the round houses are relatively small whilst those at the top and bottom of the photograph are much larger. A palstave (axe) found when a track was cut through these fields is considered to be of Bohemian type and to date between the fourteenth and twelfth century BC. (BMC 50, Cambridge University Collection of Air Photographs: copyright reserved.)*

many others, to have been laid out as far as possible at right angles to the prevailing slopes. None of the long axial boundaries continued from one end of the field-system to the other, all of them coming to a stop against one of the transverse banks, some of which were clearly laid out before the visually dominant axial examples. Some of these transverse banks appear to form a boundary around the land lying closest to the settlements. These settlements broadly consist of small numbers of dispersed round houses lying within discrete clusters and associated with a variety of small fields. The layout of the settlements appears to vary considerably and this, together with a distribution of houses which appears to bear very little relation to the main reaves, has led Fleming to suggest that the land was held not by individuals, but by the community as a whole who worked the land together. This argument would

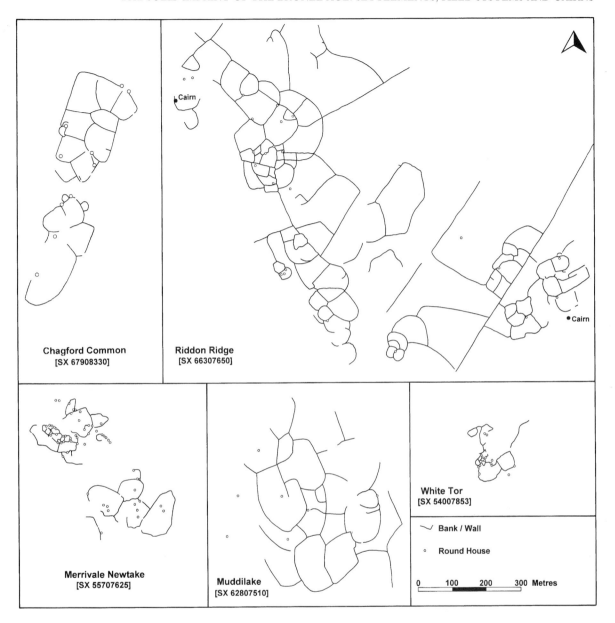

31 *Irregular aggregate field-systems vary considerably in size but all are associated with round houses. (After Butler, Ordnance Survey Antiquity Card and Author.)*

appear to be supported by the enormous size of the field-system as a whole and the lack of a track network which is really only essential if some of the land is privately owned.

Irregular aggregate field-systems are, by contrast, groups of individually shaped fields which have developed in a haphazard manner through time, perhaps in response to the need for greater arable production within parts of the moor resulting from an increase in the population of individual settlements or perhaps from exhaustion of existing land (**31**). They are much rarer and considerably less extensive than the coaxial ones. In a small number of instances, areas of irregular aggregate fields are attached to or associated with main reaves or coaxial field-systems. At Cudlipptown Down, for example, one has been attached to an earlier reave while at Riddon Ridge a block of irregular fields is clearly earlier than the nearby reave to which it has been joined by two short lengths of boundary bank. By contrast, also on Riddon Ridge another part of the irregular aggregate field-system is clearly later than the coaxial field-system which it abuts. These sites, among others, provide the evidence to support the idea that both types of fields overlapped in use. It is assumed that much the same agricultural activities were carried out within these fields as on the smaller fields surrounding the settlements within the coaxial field-systems. Intensive arable seems most likely, a situation confirmed by the build-up of lynchets along the contour boundaries, a phenomenon often indicative of arable activity. The area surrounding many of the irregular fields is generally open space with very few contemporary archaeological features and it must be assumed that these areas were used for grazing.

The third distinctive form of landscape evidence relating to the exploitation of the area are the cairnfields. These are areas where stone has been cleared and placed in heaps. Most of these are found in relatively close proximity to known settlements such as at Raddick Hill, although without excavation it is impossible to prove that there is a direct link. Most cairnfields consist of more than ten mounds, many circular in shape, although oval examples are known. In some instances, such as White Hill (North) and Homerton Hill, traces of lynchets or short lengths of rubble bank walling or even an isolated field are visible within the general area defined by the cairns (32). At other sites only cairns are visible and at White Hill (South) they form an oval-shaped ring defining an internal area measuring 120m by 60m (394ft by 197ft). Often, it is much more difficult to resolve the visible cairns into any meaningful pattern. Burials may have been placed within some of the cairns, as at Homerton Hill where a small outlying cairn contains a cist. Further examples may exist at nearby Longstone Hill where a group of sixty-four cairns lie scattered along the top of a ridge. Many are on the hill crest, where they are associated with a substantial mound and a stone which,

although now recumbent, may originally have been a standing stone. Cairnfields were probably, however, largely the result of stone clearance within areas which were not subsequently enclosed.

There are, however, examples of cairnfields lying within enclosures and a good example lies north-east of Crazy Well Pool where seventeen cairns lie within an enclosure which has incorporated at least two mounds within its circuit. The limited and localized clearance of stone was to allow for some type of agriculture. Some other types of field-system may have started life as cairnfields – with enclosure, the earlier cairns would have been removed to clear the field of obstructions and used to form boundary walls. Two cairnfields have been excavated in recent years. The one at Minehouse was excavated by the English Heritage Central Excavation Unit in advance of the construction of the Okehampton Bypass. Most of the cairns proved to be unstructured piles of rubble, confirming the clearance cairn interpretation, although one sealed a thin layer of charcoal and crushed pottery and another covered a spread of Late Neolithic pottery. The second example lay close to a settlement at Gold Park, where eight cairns were examined by Gibson in 1986. The cairns themselves included amorphous mounds of stone and no datable artefacts or a buried soil level were found.

Ritual

Archaeological evidence for ritual activity in the Bronze Age is plentiful and includes burial cairns of different types, stone circles, stone rows and standing stones. These ceremonial monuments were erected by the people living in the nearby settlements and they must have played an important role in their lives. The location of ritual monuments may impart something about the way in which the landscape was organized to meet their spiritual requirements.

Several different types of burial cairn have been identified over the years and typologies developed to classify them (33). There are, how-

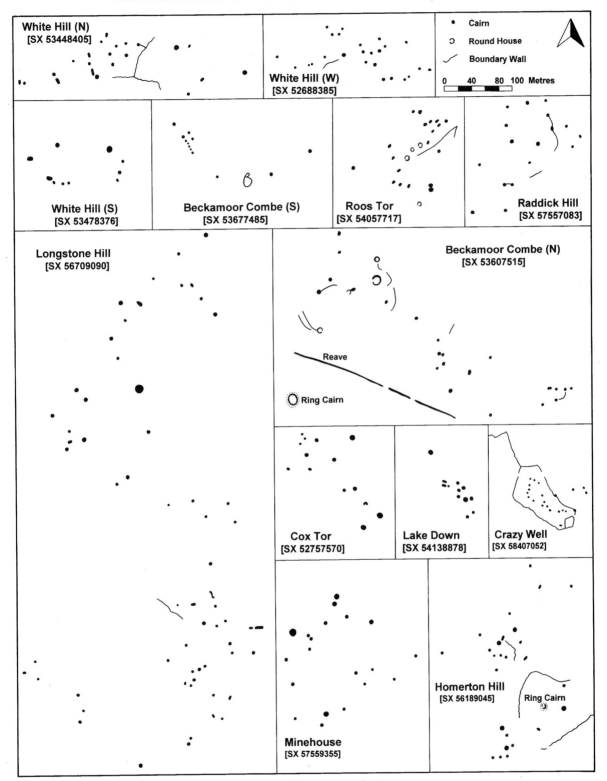

32 *Discrete clusters of small cairns are believed to indicate clearance of field stone associated with*
agricultural practice, although some of these mounds were also used to cover the dead. (Author and English Heritage.)

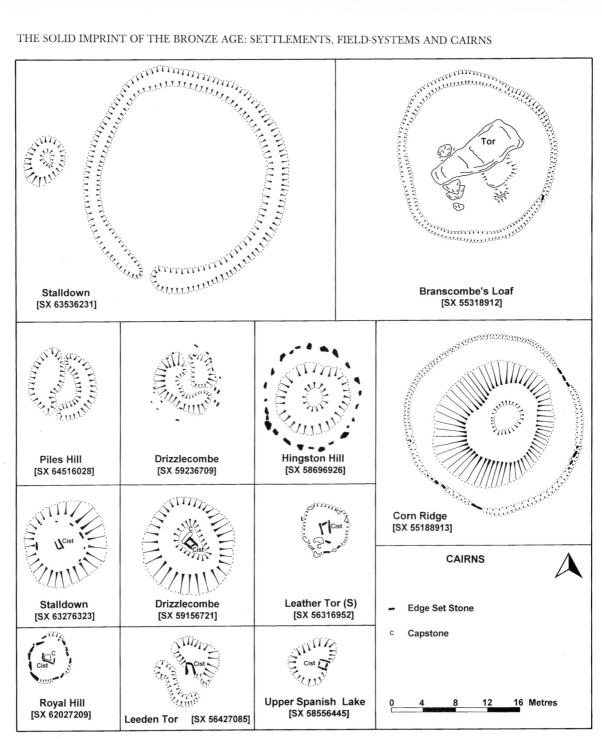

Stalldown
[SX 63536231]

Branscombe's Loaf
[SX 55318912]

Piles Hill
[SX 64516028]

Drizzlecombe
[SX 59236709]

Hingston Hill
[SX 58696926]

Corn Ridge
[SX 55188913]

Stalldown
[SX 63276323]

Drizzlecombe
[SX 59156721]

Leather Tor (S)
[SX 56316952]

CAIRNS

– **Edge Set Stone**

c **Capstone**

Royal Hill
[SX 62027209]

Leeden Tor [SX 56427085]

Upper Spanish Lake
[SX 58556445]

0   4   8   12   16 Metres

33 *A selection of cairn plans showing some of their different characteristics. (After Butler 1993, 1994 and Turner 1990.)*

ever, only two major types: round cairns and ring cairns. The latter have been subdivided by Turner into six main categories: stone rings, embanked stone circles, double kerb circles, ring settings, platform circles and encircled cairns. The situation is further complicated by excavated evidence which invariably reveals that the internal structure is much more complex than surface indications alone would suggest. Round cairns are the most numerous, with at least 1312 examples currently recorded. Generally they consist of a circular mound of stones varying in diameter from 1m to 43m (3ft 3in to 141ft) and standing between 0.1m and 4m (4in and 13ft) high. The average size of all the known cairns is however 8.83m (29ft) in diameter and 0.68m (2ft 3in) high. The hollow found in the centre of most mounds indicates robbing or partial early excavation. At over 130 cairns, edge-set stones visible around the circumference of the mound indicate the presence of a retaining kerb. Within over 116 round cairns, stone coffins known as cists have been exposed during earlier robbing and are now visible (**34**), although many others must still survive intact within the undisturbed parts of the mounds. The majority of these cists are orientated approximately north-west to south-east, and although this may have been of considerable significance to their builders, no single acceptable explanation for this phenomenon has been offered. Round cairns were erected over burials, and although many were probably placed in cists, others may have been buried in a pit dug into the subsoil, or have been inserted into an already existing mound. Two different burial practices appear to have been adopted: inhumation and cremation. Evidence for inhumation is sadly lacking because the acid soils have dissolved visible

traces of bone. However, the size of many cists strongly suggests that crouched burials of a type found elsewhere in the country did exist. Evidence for cremation burial has been found at sixteen excavated cairns where burnt bones (which are much more resistant to destruction by acid soils) are recorded normally associated with charcoal and lying within a pit. At least fifty-three cairns have produced other finds which include flint tools and arrowheads, pottery, quartz crystals, dress fasteners, bronze knives and spearheads, glass beads, cooking stones, stone hammers, a dagger pommel, rivets, a stone amulet and faience beads. A large number of these finds are considered to be Early Bronze Age (*c.* 2300–1400 BC).

Ring cairns vary considerably in character but most consist of a ring-bank of stone and earth surrounding either an open area, mound or tor outcrop (**35**). At least 212 ring cairns are known to have survived, although there are sometimes prob-

34 *The dead were often placed in stone-lined pits called cists. These are only visible where earlier cairn robbers or archaeologists have exposed them. Originally many of the cairns probably contained cists similar to this one on the northern edge of Fernworthy Reservoir. Note the capstone resting against the left hand side of the cist. The ruler is divided into 10cm intervals. (Chris Powell: copyright reserved.)*

35 *The smaller ring cairns may often be confused in the field with round houses. This structure lying within Fernworthy Reservoir is only exposed at times of drought, and prior to excavation was considered to be a round house. The excavator concluded that it was a ring cairn, but note the inner facing stones which are very similar to those found within an excavated round house on Holne Moor (see* **7**). *Their similarity in appearance may be more than a coincidence since both were built for people, except one was for the living and the other for the dead. (Chris Powell: copyright reserved.)*

lems differentiating them from either particularly badly robbed round cairns, where only the outer rim of the original mound survives, or isolated round houses. The internal diameter of ring cairns varies considerably with some being as small as 1.7m (5ft 7in) and others surviving up to 41m (134ft). The height of the ring-bank varies from as little as 0.1m (4in) to as tall as 4m (13ft). At least twelve of the ring cairns surround or are associated with a tor or large earthfast rock and these are sometimes called tor cairns. These cairns together with many round examples which are also found on or next to tors strongly suggest that they were special and may tell us something about the way in which meaning was assigned to features of the natural landscape (M. Patton, pers. comm.).

Some of the differences between cairns may be the result of recent interference rather than any original difference, and only excavation can establish the true character of a particular mound. There have been very few recent excavations of cairns, although a large number were investigated by antiquarians.

The character and distribution of cairns have been used by various writers to examine aspects of Bronze Age culture, society and land-use (**36**). Grinsell has shown that most of what he calls 'prestige' cairns (cairns with a diameter greater than 20m (65ft 8in)) lie in impressive locations from which they were clearly visible for many miles. Fleming has suggested that this blatant use of the most visually impressive locations may have been carried out to impress and inform nearby groups or newcomers that the area was already controlled and to reinforce a sense of social identity and cohesion among the communities that built them. Many of the smaller cairns are also situated in impressive locations designed to enhance their size, and these may have been used on occasion to delimit territories at a more local level. On the lower slopes of Sharpitor, west of the Stonetor Brook, and on Lee Moor groups of small cairns lying mid-way between two settlements may have been sited to denote land ownership or control. A large number of cairns are situated within the immediate vicinity of stone rows and this has been seen as a clear indication that some of the rows may have been built at this time. In more than half of the stone rows, the upper ends are denoted by a cairn, although only a few are found at the lower end. A few rows, such as those on Conies Down and Higher White Tor, do not appear to be associated with any cairns, although in these cases they may have been destroyed. At other sites such as Fernworthy, Merrivale and Stalldown many cairns survive within the vicinity of stone rows. In a large number of instances cairns are found clustered together. Five or more such mounds are defined as a cairn cemetery. No detailed analysis of the pattern of these cemeteries has yet been conducted, but many do appear to be sited in prominent locations suggesting that they too may have played a role in territorial marking. Clustering of cairns also suggests the presence of a settled population which continued to make use of the same site generation after generation. A fine example of a cairn cemetery can be seen on White Hill where at least twelve cairns including

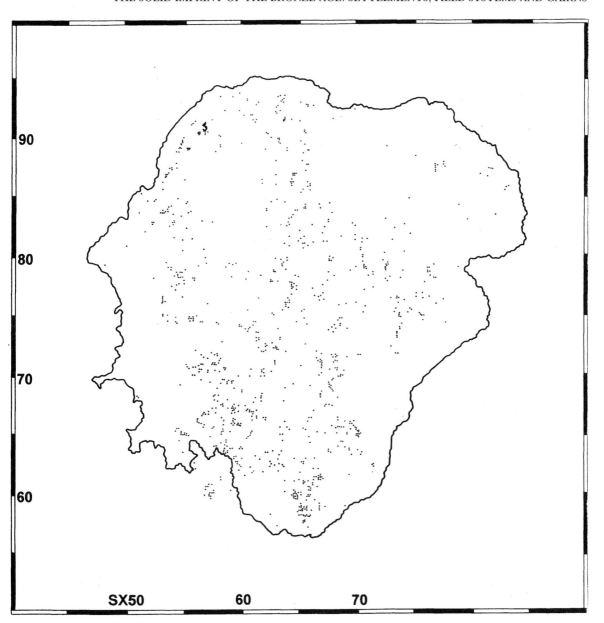

36 Within the overall pattern, linear clusters of cairns are clearly visible. The 'blank' areas on the eastern and western sides of Dartmoor represent zones of later destruction where only the most robust mounds have survived. (Source: Devon SMR.)

four-ring cairns survive in a linear arrangement reminiscent of some Wessex round-barrow cemeteries (37).

Most of the cairns lie within the upland grazing zones beyond the enclosed field-systems, and in most instances where they are found within field-systems they can be shown to be earlier, possibly built at a time when the area was used as upland grazing. There are a number of possible reasons for this situation. First, cairns may have been deliberately constructed in areas of lower economic value where they would not impinge on agricultural activities. Secondly, the cairns erected within the field-systems may have been largely destroyed by later agricultural activity. Thirdly, the upland grazing areas may have been of particular ritual

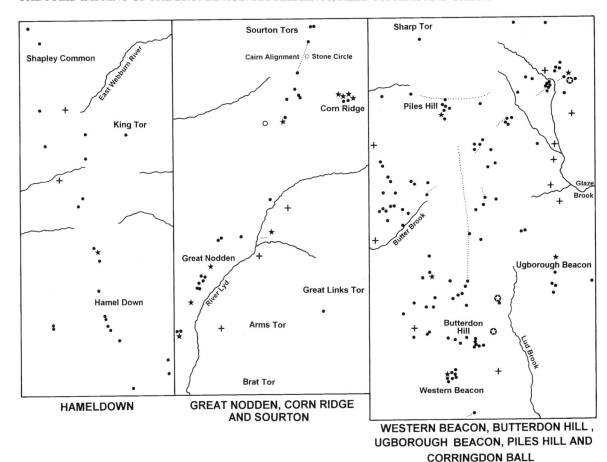

HAMELDOWN

**GREAT NODDEN, CORN RIDGE
AND SOURTON**

**WESTERN BEACON, BUTTERDON HILL,
UGBOROUGH BEACON, PILES HILL AND
CORRINGDON BALL**

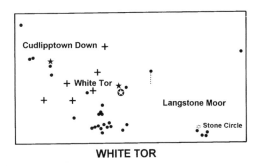

WHITE TOR

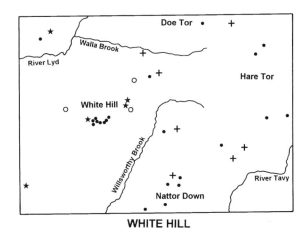

WHITE HILL

- • **Round Cairn**
- ★ **Ring Cairn**
- ○ **Cairnfield**
- ☉ **Chambered Tomb**
- ╲ **Stone Row**
- + **Settlement (> 5 houses)**

0   1   2 Kilometres

37 *Cairn cemeteries survive either as linear or nucleated clusters. The linear cemeteries on Hameldown, Great Nodden and White Hill are situated along ridges which emphasize their visual impact on the observer. The nucleated cemeteries on the other hand achieve the same result in the context of a rounded hill. In many areas containing cemeteries a discrete separation of the landscape into settlement and ritual zones is clearly visible, with the respective distributions being mutually exclusive. (Source: Devon SMR.)*

significance as a consequence of their economic importance to the society, a point emphasized perhaps by the construction of a large number of stone circles in this environment. Fourthly, there may be a religious explanation. Location on higher ground might have promoted a greater sense of closeness to gods or made them appear more spectacular. And finally, although the lower lands were clearly denoted by field boundaries, the upland areas were not. Claims on this important land may have been indicated at least in part by the building and use of cairns. Any one, none, or a combination of all five reasons may explain the preference of the cairn builders for the upland grazing zones.

Stone circles consist of a ring or rings of upright stones set around an open space and at least eighteen examples survive, although it is known that some were destroyed over the past few centuries (**38**). Identifying this class of monument in the field is more tricky than one might assume, particularly with the small ones where a slight cairn in the centre may be missed or have been destroyed in the past. The large stone circle at Brisworthy is also problematic in this respect. A low rubble bank, some 2.5m (8ft 2in) wide surrounds 75 per cent of the circumference and may indicate that this particular monument is a ring cairn. Eleven of the circles are larger than 20m (65ft 8in) in diameter, with that on Mardon Down being the largest at 38m (41ft 6in). Most of the stone circles include a single ring of uprights, but at Langstone Moor and Merrivale the monuments may have originally consisted of a second ring erected immediately outside the first. Stone circles of this type are called concentric. At Yellowmead and Shovel Down, four concentric rings of stones are found, but in both

instances care should be taken in unequivocally identifying these particular structures and it is possible that the stones were originally covered by a cairn which has since been removed.

Five stone circles were investigated by the Dartmoor Exploration Committee. These sites are Brisworthy, Down Ridge, Fernworthy and the two at Grey Wethers (**39**). At each, a layer of charcoal was found covering the old ground surface, suggesting that fire played a significant role in the ceremonies which we assume were carried out at such sites. The appearance of most stone circles today owes much to the antiquarians who re-erected many of the fallen stones and at some sites replaced those stones which were previously missing. For these reasons detailed analysis of any astronomical aspects to these sites is unlikely to be very informative.

Work by Burl and more recently by Turner has generated a number of useful ideas and observations concerning stone circles. All isolated stone circles are at a 'middle' height, that is to say they are on the near distant skyline when viewed from valleys, but from the circles themselves prominent features on the higher horizon are also clearly visible. Four of the larger circles are situated on watersheds between major rivers. These general observations may be tentatively extended to suggest that the stone circles were erected within an open environment and that an impressive vista to and from the circle was essential. The date of the Dartmoor stone circles remains uncertain, although their association with cairns of Bronze Age date suggests that a similar date can be inferred. Burl notes that these stone circles are relatively small compared with examples in other areas and he believes this may be because they are late in date or because they were built and used by smaller communities.

Standing stones or 'menhirs' are single upright slabs and are usually very difficult to date, although examples in the south-west are known to have been associated with Bronze Age material. There are only two definite isolated standing stones (Beardown Man and Harbourne Head) together with a number of others, over which

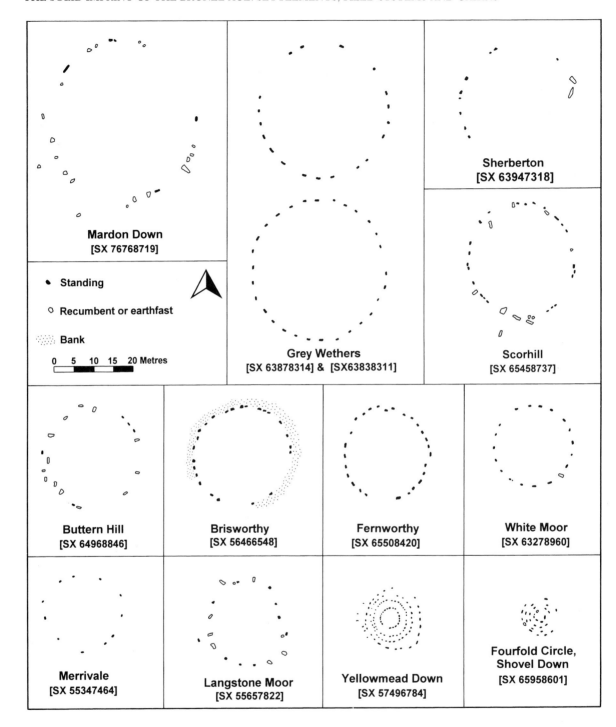

38 *This selection of stone circle plans includes a number of sites which although they are often referred to as stone circles may in fact belong to different categories of site. The multiple circles at Yellowmead Down and Fourfold Circle may be robbed round cairns, while the survival of a low bank around the circle at Brisworthy may suggest that it is a ring cairn. (After Butler 1991a, 1991b, 1994; Fletcher et al. 1974b; OS Antiquity Cards; Worth 1981.)*

doubts exist about their prehistoric origin. The White Moor Stone near a stone circle of the same name and the Hanging Stone on Lee Moor may be standing stones still in their original location although both have been re-used as boundary stones. The stone on the southern slopes of Leeden Tor and another within Merrivale Newtake may also be later marker stones. There are possible standing stones at Halstock and Butterdon Down, while on Mardon Down an upright stone called the Headless Cross is now considered to be a menhir as are some other medieval wayside crosses which may be re-used standing stones. A number of now-recumbent stones are also believed to have once stood during the prehistoric period. Among these are large slabs on Longstone Hill and Sharp Tor. Finally, the field name Great Longstone at Gorselands may imply that a stone once stood in this area.

Standing stones are somewhat enigmatic. It has been suggested that they served a variety of functions as way markers, territorial markers, grave and cemetery markers, meeting places and as a focus for ritual activity.

The surviving ritual monuments are tangible evidence of the importance of spiritual and religious experience in the past. They seem enigmatic to the casual observer and retain an element of hushed reverence to a ceremonial and symbolic heritage that we do not fully comprehend.

39 *The Scorhill stone circle is one of seven in this part of the moor and the relatively regular spacing between them has led writers to suggest that they formed part of some grand design. (Paul Rendell: copyright reserved.)*

However, the significance of the social organization, planning, design and logistical problems, which the erection of such structures represents, does translate through time and still holds relevance today. Of the ceremonial, we may only imaginatively speculate (**colour plate 6**).

Tinworking

Industrial activities, including metalworking, pottery production and flint knapping, were also carried out during the Bronze Age. Most appear to have left little trace on the landscape and, for this reason, need not detain us any further. There is, however, one industry which at the time probably did have an impact on the character of the landscape: the exploitation of tin. Although later reworking of earlier tinworks has probably obliterated much of the physical evidence, it is worthwhile examining the character of this significant activity.

Tin alloyed with copper produces bronze: it is therefore assumed that from the time bronze became widely used in Britain there must have been an interest in the tin deposits of south-west England. There are no positively identified prehistoric tinwork or smelting sites known on Dartmoor, and much of the discussion has necessarily centred around inferential information. No scholar has yet concluded that tin was definitely not exploited during the Bronze Age, but some difference of opinion concerning the scale and the impact of the industry on the landscape does exist. The lack of positive evidence to indicate the level of tinworking during prehistoric times is at variance with nearby Cornwall where large numbers of artefacts indicating a significant level of interest in the tin-bearing ground have been recovered. The scarcity of such finds from Dartmoor is a reflection, not of any paucity of prehistoric activity but rather of more recent activity in Cornwall. There, many of the earlier streamworks were reworked during the nineteenth century and it was during this last phase of exploitation that many artefacts were found and often reported by Cornish antiquarians. On Dartmoor at this time, however, there was no systematic reworking of earlier streamworks and as a result finds were not exposed. The only exceptions to this are at Headland Girt, Vitifer and Tavistock where prehistoric artefacts were found in old mines, though information relating to the precise position of these finds was sadly not recorded. Material indicating prehistoric exploitation of the local tin deposits, which has been recovered under more stringent archaeological conditions, has been reported only from the excavations of the Bronze Age settlement on Dean Moor by Fox. Excavations in advance of the Avon Reservoir led to recovery of a piece of tin ore (cassiterite) from House 5B and more significantly a globule of smelted tin from House 7. These finds certainly support the idea that the occupants of this settlement were interested in the nearby tin deposits. Two other round houses which contained either tin slag or ore are recorded in the literature. One at Yes Tor Bottom and another at Fernworthy also contained medieval or post-medieval pottery, and Worth, who excavated both sites, concluded that the slag and ore belonged to the historic period.

It must be significant that despite the excavation of a large number of round houses only two contained evidence relating to tinworking. The reason for this is probably that the processing of the tin was carried out immediately next to the tinworks and certainly at some distance from the settlement. This situation should not be unexpected since, in the historic period, the ores are known to have been crushed and smelted in purpose-built structures situated next to the tinworks and not taken to the settlements to be processed.

Further inferential evidence for prehistoric tinworking is suggested by the decline in alder pollen at Wotter Common on south-west Dartmoor, which Beckett has argued could have resulted from tin-streaming activities, though other possible explanations do exist. Penhallurick has suggested that seven faience beads found at Shaugh Moor were made from local china clay and that they were a by-product of tinworking in the area.

Conclusion

The changes wrought upon the Bronze Age landscape of Dartmoor are remarkable in many ways. The wealth of available archaeological evidence means that this is the earliest period in prehistory which can be properly understood in any detail. We can infer a good deal about territorial boundaries, farming practices, industry, housing and ritual, although some aspects still remain elusive and a matter for conjecture. The richness of this fossilized landscape should not be underestimated. However, we must also remember that structures only survive here because they have not been systematically obliterated or masked by subsequent agrarian or industrial practice, as has happened in lowland areas. Perhaps the treatment of the uplands was always different, just as it is today; we must be careful not to imagine the same practices were automatically carried out in the lowlands. However, we are still able to perceive and appreciate the changes and developments in communication, agriculture, housing and culture which the archaeology of the period graphically represents. The innovations of the Neolithic were now being realized, elaborated and embellished in many ways.

4

Dartmoor's dark ages: the Iron Age to the Early Christian era

Iron Age (700 BC–AD 43)

Relative to the dramatic evidence from the Bronze Age, subsequent periods are rather poorly represented in the archaeological record. In landscape terms, one positive aspect of this is that significant tracts of the earlier landscape have remained largely undisturbed for centuries and these are now yielding up some of their secrets to archaeological investigation. However, realistically the Iron Age would seem to represent a somewhat catastrophic change in the fortunes of the upland inhabitants. Current evidence indicates the abandonment of previously populated areas, with habitation being relegated to an unknown number of settlements on the moorland fringe. Summer grazing on the uplands appears to have continued and been extended to areas which were previously more intensively farmed.

The evidence of Iron Age occupation in the middle of the moor is both fragmentary and limited to a small number of sites. Only at the settlement sites of Kestor, Foale's Arrishes, Fernworthy and Gold Park has excavated evidence been recovered. At Kestor, excavations by Fox of a large round house lying within a circular enclosure known as Round Pound revealed a complex site which, although established in the Bronze Age, also contained a few sherds of early Iron Age pottery. Most significant, however, was the discovery of a small iron-smelting furnace and forging pit which the excavator considered also to be of Iron Age date. Unfortunately, there is also evidence of medieval activity at this site, which

has led some archaeologists to challenge Fox's dating of the ironworking. Pollen analysis of a soil sample taken from the East Field at Kestor suggests that following an initial period of cultivation this field lay barren for a number of years before being brought back under the plough. It is tempting to link the first phase of cultivation with the Bronze Age and the second with the Iron Age, although unfortunately the evidence is too imprecise to confirm such an attractive conclusion.

Excavation of another house lying within a small enclosure at Foale's Arrishes recovered pottery sherds which have been assigned to either late Bronze Age or early Iron Age vessels. At Fernworthy, Worth's excavation of the largest house within the settlement yielded several sherds of pottery which may belong to the Iron Age, although once again this building was certainly occupied during the Bronze Age. The final settlement site to have produced evidence of Iron Age activity is at Gold Park, where excavations carried out by Gibson between 1984 and 1986 revealed a number of timber structures lying below later cairns and a timber round house superseded by a stone one. Radiocarbon dates suggest that the two round houses both belonged to the later part of the Iron Age, and although these dates may be questioned, the recovery of a small number of late Iron Age La Tène pottery sherds would appear to confirm this date.

A small number of stray finds from the moor confirm that the area was not abandoned during this time. A hoard of twelve currency bars from

Holne Chase, a sherd of pottery from Cator, two Greek coins from Court Farm in Holne parish and a gold coin known as a stater from Bellever Tor are all indicative of some degree of continued interest in the rich upland pasture. Over vast tracts of the higher moorland, however, no Iron Age material or structures have yet been found and this would certainly point to less intensive activity here than during the preceding Bronze Age.

In the lowlands and moorland fringes, however, there is abundant evidence of Iron Age occupation. For example at least twelve hillforts and a similar number of enclosed settlements survive. At one site on Hunter's Tor, recent work by Silvester and Quinnell has revealed two major phases of hillfort construction, one of which was never completed, overlying an earlier field-system (**40**). The location of some hillforts implies the continued use

of the nearby moorland. The three most strongly defended forts are at Hembury, Brentor and Cranbrook (**41**). In these cases, strategic locations have been fortified by the addition of ramparts and ditches. Other sites appear to be less well-fortified or positioned. These may have been primarily used for the protection of livestock which were grazed on the neighbouring moorland. Of these the most sophisticated is Wooston Castle which has up to four lines of defences.

Obviously Dartmoor was never wholly abandoned during this period, but the shift in emphasis from upland to lowland occupation is a significant change. The reasons for this marked shift in land-use are complex and a number of interrelated factors are considered to be responsible. Foremost among these may be climatic deterioration – increasingly cold and wet conditions – which in

40 *The complex multi-phase hillfort at Hunter's Tor overlies an earlier field-system. (Photograph Frances Griffith, Devon County Council: copyright reserved.)*

41 *Hillforts were built to utilize the local topography and this explains in part the variety of plans. (After OS Antiquity Cards and Collis 1972.)*

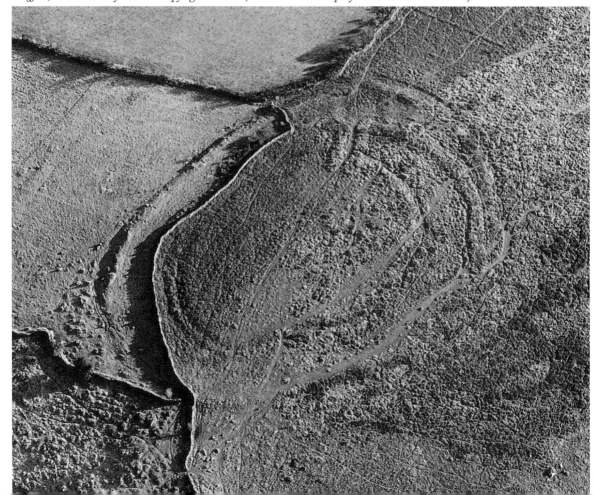

1 *Grimspound and Headland Warren. This complex palimpsest may be viewed from the most visited archaeological monument on Dartmoor. In the foreground are round houses lying within Grimspound. In the middle distance to the left is part of the Challacombe medieval field-system and to the right of this are post-medieval openworks and leats within Headland Warren.* (Author.)

2 *Re-excavation of this longhouse at Hutholes during 1994 has led to reassessment of many conclusions reached by the original excavator.* (Exeter Museums Archaeological Field Unit: copyright reserved.)

3 *In the pale evening light, the successful hunting party returns to the encampment where the meal will be prepared. Against a backdrop of scorched earth, and with acrid smoke in the air, newly made implements will be added to the hunters' kit while any by-products from the carcass will provide raw materials for clothing and more tools. In the months to come the newly burnt woodland will provide fresh and luxuriant grazing for the deer and other animals on which these people rely.* (Chris Powell: copyright reserved.)

4 *Neolithic society was complex. The major ritual, defence and funerary monuments represent a high degree of social interaction and co-operation. Daily life, by contrast, assumed a more humble scale: stones were cleared to facilitate basic agricultural practices, dwellings were constructed and everyday items such as pots and tools were manufactured.* (Chris Powell: copyright reserved.)

5 *The significant impact of the human populace upon a scene which today is merely ruinous helps the observer to imagine the area alive. The dry-stone walls of the Bronze Age settlement at Grimspound bear witness to a bustling community, typical of many found throughout the moor.* (Chris Powell: copyright reserved.)

6 *The staggering array of ritual monuments associated with Merrivale indicates the strategic and spiritual importance of this area to those people who lived within its influence. Although the ceremonies may be lost to the modern observer,* *we cannot help but appreciate the measure of planning, motivation, organization and logistical preparation which produced this complex of sites.* (Chris Powell: copyright reserved.)

7 *This probable Early Christian memorial stone now standing on the village green at Sourton was found built into a barn and moved in recent years to its present location.* (Paul Rendell: copyright reserved.)

8 *The hamlet at Houndtor epitomizes medieval existence on the upland marginal lands. The fields near to the farms were intensively used and the encroaching moorland kept at bay by stone walls and hard physical work. Despite the conditions, success was possible albeit hard-won.* (Chris Powell: copyright reserved.)

9 *Streaming for tin. Extracting the highly prized tin involved initiative, enterprise, determination, forward planning, toil, skill, fortitude and luck. Not only was the work physically demanding but it also required mathematical and engineering genius.* (Chris Powell: copyright reserved.)

10 *The significance of peat for a variety of uses, including heating and charcoal production, has long been appreciated. The logistics of moving the people to and removing peat from the source were as complicated as any encountered on the moor. As a general rule of thumb, the best peat came from the most isolated and inaccessible places.* (Chris Powell: copyright reserved.)

11 *In neighbouring Cornwall large numbers of impressive engine-houses lie scattered throughout the metalliferous regions. On Dartmoor the only well-preserved engine-house stands at Wheal Betsy adjacent to Job's Shaft.* (Author.)

12 *Bronze Age hunting, farming, construction techniques, ritual activity and daily life or death are graphically illustrated at Stanlake. The quantity of archaeological evidence attests to a community bursting with vitality and fortitude, and a population determined to succeed.* (Chris Powell: copyright reserved.)

13 *The population might have dwindled somewhat but Stanlake remained a workable enterprise. Farming was intensive, construction techniques and housing had drastically changed and tinworking was now an essential and providential diversification to farming.* (Chris Powell: copyright reserved.)

14 *One of the earlier farms abandoned during the latter part of the medieval period remains deserted and the whole area is now farmed from the one remaining Stanlake farmstead. Tin streaming in the valley has also ceased as the deposits have become exhausted. The new leat serving the growing town of Devonport now cuts through the fields and the presence of a surveyor attests to significant developments in the scientific and engineering technology now utilized.* (Chris Powell: copyright reserved.)

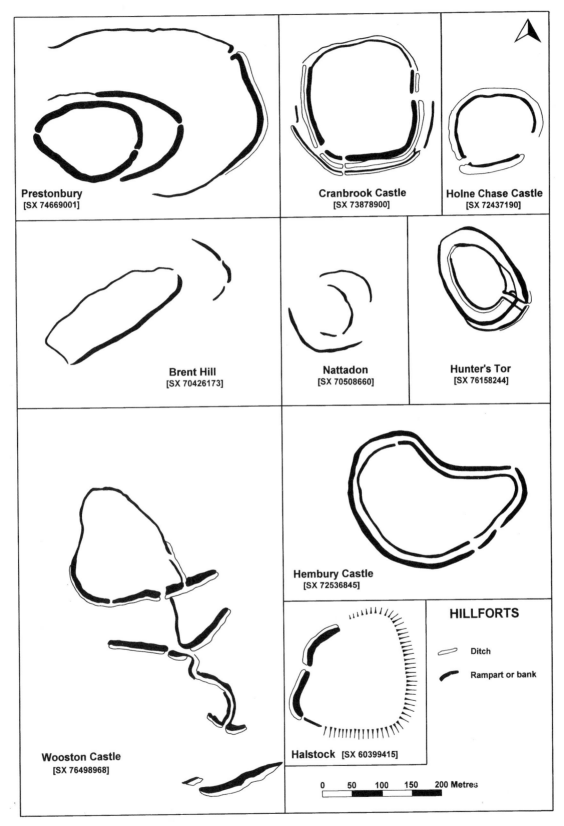

Prestonbury
[SX 74669001]

Cranbrook Castle
[SX 73878900]

Holne Chase Castle
[SX 72437190]

Brent Hill
[SX 70426173]

Nattadon
[SX 70508660]

Hunter's Tor
[SX 76158244]

Hembury Castle
[SX 72536845]

Wooston Castle
[SX 76498968]

Halstock [SX 60399415]

HILLFORTS

Ditch

Rampart or bank

0   50   100   150   200 Metres

the first instance meant that crops at higher altitudes did not ripen as before. The increased rainfall combined perhaps with overcropping and insufficient manuring led to podzolization of the soils, resulting in a loss of nutrients and the development of acid peaty soils which were no longer suitable for arable farming. The consequence of this can be seen in the pollen record: samples from Taw Head and Rattlebrook on the high moorland show lower levels of bracken, plantains and other weeds associated with cultivation so suggesting a period of reduced human pressure. Some workers, including Simmons, have suggested that primary woodland in the lowlands was subject to extensive clearance at this time, but others believe that in general terms only those areas previously cleared were cultivated. Evidence to support both approaches exists and the answer may be a combination of the two, with for example clearance being limited to a small number of discrete areas surrounding the moorland.

Roman era (AD 43–410)

In contrast to many other parts of southern Britain, the evidence for Roman occupation is almost non-existent. It may be said that 'Veni, Vidi, Vici' never resounded across the moors from a Roman throat. Features or structures definitely related to this period are unknown. This is particularly curious given the known Roman interest in tin and other minerals elsewhere in Europe. It seems extremely unlikely that such a large area of varied natural resources should have gone unexploited for so long. Roman occupation of other upland areas is also well known, so climatic or topographic factors cannot have been significant. The only tangible evidence for Roman interest comes from a small number of artefacts. The most notable are a hoard of about 200 coins dating from early in the fourth century AD on East Hill, above Okehampton; four coins from a crevice on Black Tor, Walkhampton; a coin dug up in Princetown in 1885 and a glass bead from Watern Oke, which may be of a Roman type.

However, within the lowland areas immediately adjacent to the moor, significant quantities of Roman material and even some structures have been identified and these include lengths of road around the northern, eastern and western edges; at least one possible signal-tower platform at Sourton; forts at Okehampton and North Tawton; fortlets at Okehampton and in Ide parish; settlements; a number of coin hoards and other stray finds. The evidence thus points to relatively intensive use of the areas bordering Dartmoor during the Roman period – and in all likelihood the higher moorland was also being exploited, though in ways which have left a minimal impact.

Early Christian era (AD 410–1066)

There is no archaeological evidence for intensive activity on the high moorland at this time. Only three sites have been claimed as belonging to this period, and in each instance this dating has been challenged. The first two are at the medieval settlements of Hound Tor and Hutholes, which were excavated by Minter between 1961 and 1975. It has been suggested that settlements were established at both sites in the seventh or eighth centuries AD. The evidence included a complex series of stake holes which were resolved by the excavators into a sequence of turf buildings, which were then each assumed to have had a life of around thirty years, giving a particularly early date. There are two fundamental problems with this hypothesis. First, there is no evidence to support the thirty-year replacement date and, more significantly, a recent re-excavation of one of the longhouses at Hutholes could not locate any of the turf building stake holes (see **colour plate 2**). The third site where an Early Christian date has been claimed is Week Ford, where charcoal collected from an exposed layer rich in tin slag has been dated by radiocarbon to between AD 570 and AD 890. The use of a single date from a potentially contaminated context to demonstrate early tin processing at a site where considerable activity is known from later periods cannot be counted as conclusive.

Around the fringes of the moor the evidence for activity is more abundant although by no means plentiful. The most important single site is

the burh at Lydford on the western side of Dartmoor. The origins of the settlement cannot be determined with certainty, although the dedication of the local church to St Petrock may suggest foundation early in the seventh century. Certainly by AD 900 the settlement was important enough to be provided with fortifications, one of only four towns or burhs in Devon. Nearly 100 years later, in AD 997 the defences were strong enough to repulse an attack by the Danes. The line of the Saxon town defences and the internal street layout is clearly fossilized in the present-day town and limited excavation has confirmed their date, character and importance (**42**).

Much of the evidence from this time relates to religious sites, and these include the Saxon

42 *Aerial photograph of Lydford. Despite centuries of continual occupation, the outline of the Anglo-Saxon town and its street plan are clearly visible. Within the town the later ringwork, castle and church form distinctive landmarks. (Photograph Frances Griffith, Devon County Council: copyright reserved.)*

Benedictine abbey at Buckfast founded in 1018 by Cnut and the abbey of St Mary and St Rumon at Tavistock which was begun in AD 971 and burnt down by the same Danes who attacked Lydford in AD 997. At South Brent, Saxon stonework survives within the belfry of the later church. A small number of churches lying a short distance from the moor have Celtic dedications and were possibly founded during this period. Examples are the parish churches of St Bridget at Bridestowe and St Constantine at Milton Abbot.

A small number of inscribed memorial stones bear further witness to activity around the fringes of the moor. The four stones at Tavistock, Buckland Monachorum, East Ogwell and Lustleigh lie within churchyards and indicate that these particular religious centres had been established by this time. The remainder appear to lie at the interface between the moorland and enclosed land, often situated on routeways. This siting may point to an interest in the moorland. Amongst these stones are two at Sourton (**colour plate 7**), and those at Roborough Down and Fardel in Cornwood parish and a possible example at Ilsington.

Documentation has a part to play in our understanding of the later Early Christian landscape and, for the first time, information concerning the extent and location of a few estates and the names of a few settlements are known. The settlement at Treable is recorded in AD 976 and the place name 'Christow', which means a place hallowed by Christian association, has led Pearce to suggest a seventh-century origin. Most important are two charters which record the boundaries of land given by the crown. The Meavy Charter (1031) describes the boundary of a block of land given by Cnut to his thegn. The estate boundary follows the line of Buckland Monachorum parish boundary but ignores those of Meavy, Sheepstor and Walkhampton. This would appear to suggest that although the boundaries of Buckland Monachorum had already been defined those of the other three adjacent parishes had not. The charter also refers to an existing 'highway of the dwellers of Buckland' which would appear to have been a clearly defined access route to the high moorland. Thus, although there is no archaeological evidence to support the idea that the upper moorland continued to be exploited at this time, the documentary evidence indicates clearly that this important grazing resource was not being wasted. The Peadington Charter (1050) defines a substantial new estate centred on the modern parishes of Widecombe, Buckland and

Ashburton. Again, the parish boundaries of the lower-lying parishes are respected by this new estate, though those of Widecombe, Manaton and Ilsington are ignored. Together these charters appear to represent an expansion of organized land-use into the area between the high moor and old established estates. It would not seem unreasonable to assume that archaeological evidence for this documented expansion survives within these areas, but sadly it has yet to be recognized.

This is the first period in which documentary evidence is available to aid our study of the landscape and comfortably it appears, in the main, to complement the picture derived from the archaeological record, with the fringes being permanently settled and the upper moors being used for seasonal grazing.

Conclusion

The period covered by this chapter represents some 1800 years during which the archaeological record is currently very sparse. Compared with both previous and subsequent periods, the archaeologist is struggling to locate the evidence for activity. The situation in the surrounding lowlands is slightly improved and here documentary research, excavation and, more importantly, aerial photographic work, particularly by Frances Griffith of Devon County Council, has in recent years demonstrated the character of the activity in these areas. By contrast, the evidence from the moor would suggest that permanent settlements were not a feature during this time, but it would be wrong to see the moor as being abandoned. Transhumance must have continued to play an important role in the area's economy, and the character of the surrounding lowland's settlement pattern and economy must therefore have been influenced by the proximity of this large and important upland grazing resource. The interrelationship between the upland and surrounding lowlands is known to be a complex one, and at all periods the influence of the rest of south-west England – and at times even parts of Europe and the rest of the world – has had profound effects on the nature of land-use and ultimately the archaeology.

5
Medieval Dartmoor: a hive of industry

The medieval period (AD 1066–1500) is the first period for which a large quantity of contemporary documentation is available to complement our understanding of the visible archaeology. It represents a time of intensive use after a hiatus of several centuries which left very few traces. Compared with the prehistoric period, however, the surviving medieval archaeology may at first glance appear disappointing, particularly when compared with areas of the country such as Yorkshire and the English Midlands where extensive and well-preserved medieval landscapes are known. But, detailed examination of the many diverse components of Dartmoor's medieval landscape rapidly dispels this illusion and reveals a complex array of different types of site together producing an informative picture of life, death, agriculture and industry.

Settlement

Medieval settlements are significantly different to the prehistoric ones. Medieval buildings are generally rectangular in shape while their prehistoric predecessors are circular. Medieval settlements form a dispersed pattern of farmsteads and hamlets, while many prehistoric settlements form large nucleated clusters of buildings (**43**). Many of the medieval settlements remain in occupation today and although altered and modified by later generations some of the original buildings remain identifiable and are of considerable architectural importance. Other settlements continued in use into the post-medieval period only to be abandoned later, while some were deserted during medieval times and never re-occupied. Each form of surviving settlement has important information to offer the archaeologist.

Over 130 deserted medieval settlements are known, and while many are single abandoned farms, the majority are hamlets containing between two and six farmhouses. Documentary and archaeological evidence indicates that most of these settlements were probably established between the twelfth and mid-fourteenth centuries. The expansion of settlements and arable farming into less hospitable parts of the moor appears to be the result of land pressures caused by an increasing population, combined with climatic conditions which made arable farming at higher altitudes possible, if risky. These settlements generally lie within the current moorland fringe and survive as clusters of small buildings including at least one longhouse, ancillary buildings and a number of small plots which served as kitchen gardens or stock pens. Longhouses are through-passage, rectangular, dual-purpose buildings in which domestic and animal accommodation was provided under one roof. Surrounding many of these settlements are the associated fossilized field-systems. Several settlements have been excavated in recent years, and the results of this work together with detailed field survey and documentary analysis have been most informative. The settlements at Hound Tor, Hutholes and Dinna Clerks were excavated by Minter between 1961 and 1975

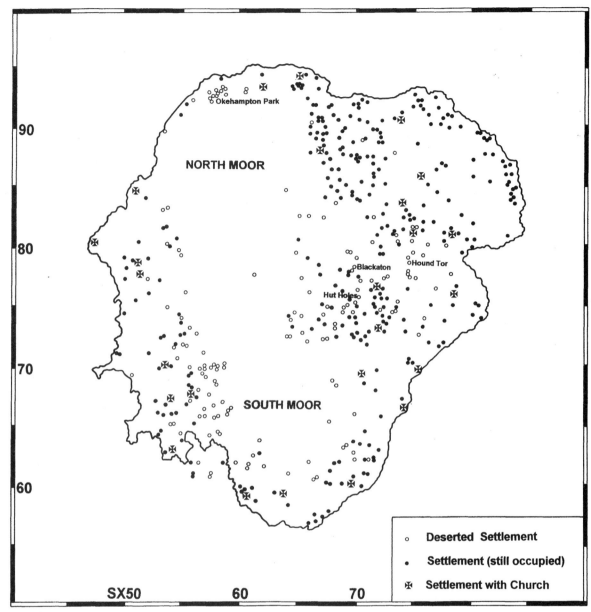

43 *This distribution of medieval settlements is derived from archaeological and historical sources. Most of the deserted settlements lie within moorland or fringe farmland, while most of the lower lying farms continue in use today. (Source: Devon SMR.)*

(**44**). At Hound Tor two separate settlements were excavated and found to be broadly contemporary. The northern site includes a farmstead with a longhouse, two ancillary buildings and garden plots lying within a prehistoric enclosed

settlement. Both prehistoric round houses were re-used, with one being modified to form a small barn and the other being converted to an animal pen. The southern settlement at Hound Tor is often referred to as a village but given that it comprises four longhouses and seven ancillary buildings it should be regarded as a hamlet.

Details concerning the development of the settlement were revealed by excavation (**colour plate 8**). One longhouse was enlarged by the addition of a second inner room, lean-to and porch. In

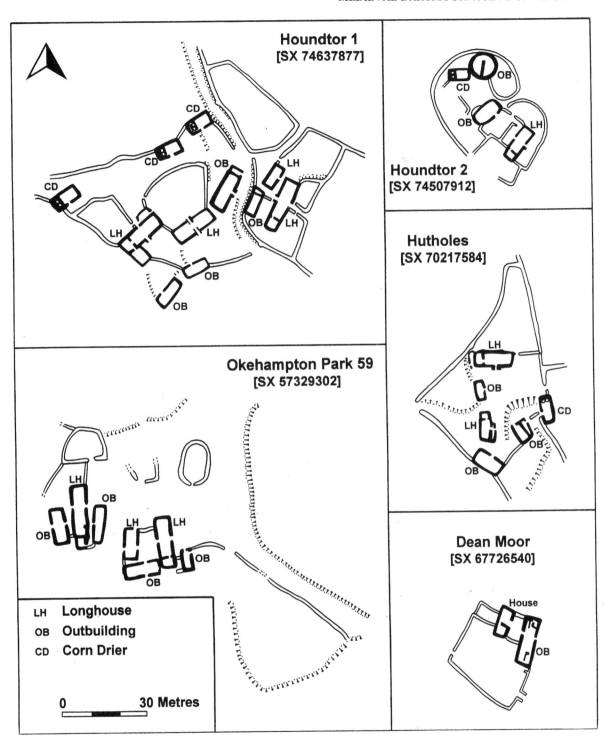

Houndtor 1
[SX 74637877]

Houndtor 2
[SX 74507912]

Hutholes
[SX 70217584]

Okehampton Park 59
[SX 57329302]

Dean Moor
[SX 67726540]

House

LH   **Longhouse**
OB   **Outbuilding**
CD · **Corn Drier**

0   30 Metres

44 *Five deserted medieval settlements have been excavated. The settlement at Okehampton Park was investigated prior to its destruction, while the one on Dean Moor lies within the Avon Reservoir and is only visible during droughts. The remaining three were investigated as part of a research programme and remain available for inspection. (After Austin 1985 and Fox 1958.)*

another, partition walls which divided the byre from the living quarters were added, possibly at the same time as two porches. Another building which started life as a longhouse was later converted to a barn when one door was blocked, the original byre floor was lowered and a lean-to was added. The conversion of this house into a barn reduced the number of longhouses within the settlement to three. It is reasonable to assume that the three corn driers were built around this time to serve the three remaining farms. The installation of corn driers towards the end of the settlement's life strongly suggests increasingly wet summers which meant that the oat crop was not ripening as before, and this situation may have led to the eventual abandonment of the first longhouse. Beresford suggests that continued deterioration of the climate was probably responsible for an increased frequency of crop failures and animal disease, leading ultimately to the desertion of the whole settlement in the middle of the fourteenth century. Given this timescale it should be noted that the Black Death may also have been a contributory factor for abandonment.

The smaller settlement at Hutholes includes two longhouses, three outbuildings and a corn drier. Austin has suggested that this group of buildings represents a single farmstead, an argument certainly supported by the presence of only one corn drier. Again the effect of climatic deterioration on agriculture is seen as the most likely explanation for desertion around 1350. The settlement at Dinna Clerks differs from the others in that only the longhouse survives and no information concerning the nature of associated ancillary buildings is known. Excavation revealed that the farm had been built around 1200 and succumbed to a catastrophic fire about 100 years later. The large number of artefacts recovered from this building, together with a Henry III Long Cross penny found within the doorway, confirm the hurried departure of its inhabitants.

A cluster of at least eight discrete deserted settlements associated with a well-preserved field-system and complex of trackways lie within Okehampton Deer Park. The reason for desertion this time may

be different and Austin has argued, using documentary evidence, that the tenant farmers in this area known as Byrham were evicted by Hugh de Courtenay in around 1300 to make way for his deer park (45). Although a disaster for the inhabitants, the result was the creation of a fossilized medieval landscape, which remained unaltered until modern enclosures were added sometime after 1780.

The excavations carried out within Okehampton Park by Austin between 1976 and 1978 were directed towards the western settlement which was threatened by quarrying. This settlement included seven stone buildings, related enclosures and evidence of earlier timber structures. The largest timber building was probably built in the first half of the twelfth century and lay directly beneath one of the later stone longhouses. The stone buildings included two principal longhouses, one smaller longhouse and four ancillary buildings. Within the byres of the longhouses, lines of stake holes found running parallel to the long wall of the building were interpreted as hay rack supports and in one a series of stake holes lying at right angles to the wall was believed to represent the remnants of stalls. A number of other stake holes found within the living quarters are believed to be the result of internal furnishings.

Considerable discussion concerning the reasons for settlement desertion has led to a number of possible explanations. Among these are deteriorating climate, declining soil fertility, disease and the introduction of sheep farming. Desertion was, however, not universal and many settlements remain in occupation to the present day. An attractive explanation for the apparent haphazard nature of the desertion has been offered by Austin who suggests that differences in tenurial holding may have been responsible, with those settlements built and occupied by bond tenants being abandoned while those belonging to freeholders remained in use.

Although our knowledge of early longhouses comes from excavated examples, the longhouse as a building tradition persisted until the seventeenth century, despite going through several changes. Of those still standing, many date back to the fifteenth century, and as a style are perfectly adapted to the rigours imposed by a harsh climate. They huddle on the hillsides, are long, low and trend downslope. They were still used as combined house and cattle stall but most have been adapted down the years with a gradual pronounced separation of the domestic and animal quarters.

The central hearth was replaced by a substantial chimney often backing onto the cross passage, but not exclusively so. Additional upper rooms were inserted over the hall to maximize space available without having to alter the original roofline. External extensions used as kitchens and parlours often blocked one end of the passage. Internal stud walls and screens which formed the partitions were replaced with stone, or even built in stone from the outset. Another innovation was the construction of exterior doors

directly to the byre, although the entrance via the cross passage was usually maintained, often as a feeding walk. The large hall was subdivided, and because the roof was so high upper storeys were inserted as at Hill, Christow. By the sixteenth or seventeenth century, many were being constructed with an upper floor.

The later longhouse was often a splendid structure, with ornate carved interior and exterior woodwork, stone mouldings, mullioned windows, and elaborate chimneys. They were constructed from dressed granite and unlike their dry-stone predecessors were mortared. Eventually, domestic quarters overtook the byre and cattle were moved

45 *A particularly well-preserved medieval agricultural landscape survives within Okehampton Park, where the outlines of several farmsteads linked together by tracks and each surrounded by narrow strip fields are clearly visible. (David Austin: copyright reserved.)*

46 *The late medieval longhouse at Sanders in the hamlet of Lettaford contains original roof trusses, a large porch and is partly built with substantial ashlar granite blocks. (Chris Powell: copyright reserved.)*

to separate accommodation. As a result, by the end of the seventeenth century, the longhouse in its truest sense of animal and human shelter had ceased. There are many surviving longhouses but among the more notable examples are Higher Uppacott, Poundsgate; Hole Farm, Chagford; Higher Shilstone, Throwleigh; and Sanders, Lettaford, North Bovey (**46**).

Although, undoubtedly the most celebrated of building styles, the longhouse was not alone. Its immediate contemporary was the two- or three-celled 'through-passage house'. This style also developed through time and, like the longhouse, had a hall which was divided from service rooms by a through passage, often located at the lower end of the house. The development of the chimney allowed layouts to change drastically. The through-passage houses developed from open halls to two-storied structures during the sixteenth century. Kitchens were often detached, freestanding structures (because of the potential fire risk) until the development of stone hearths and smoking chambers. Kitchens were added to existing buildings during the seventeenth century. Extensions of additional rooms like parlours and dairies also appeared.

Many of the earliest two-storeyed houses had only one cell, and a good example still stands at Yeo Farm, Chagford. There is also evidence for so-called 'first floor halls'. One of the earliest examples at Neadon, Manaton, dates to the late fifteenth century. The upper floor had a hall and

solar (living room), while the lower floor had a wide door and was used for storage.

Within many villages and towns on the lower ground surrounding the moor, medieval buildings still survive and the present settlement layout reflects their medieval origins. At South Zeal the original layout of the town is particularly well preserved, with the original narrow burgage plots remaining remarkably intact (**47**).

Field-systems

Most of the deserted settlements lie within well-preserved contemporary field-systems. These vary considerably in form. At some farms, earlier prehistoric fields were brought back into production, while more often a series of small, irregular-shaped fields were constructed. The open-field systems, found in lowland areas of Britain are rare, but a fine example can be seen at Challacombe where a large number of long, narrow fields defined by banks and lynchets can be seen (**48**). The lynchets comprise steep linear breaks in the slope which were formed by erosion and soil build-up caused by ploughing. Other examples of strip fields have been noted at Godsworthy, Stanlake and on Holne Moor (**49**). Within many of the strip fields and the more numerous small irregular fields traces of ridge and furrow can be seen. Ridge and furrow survives as a series of parallel banks and hollows, formed by cultivation, usually ploughing though occasionally hand-digging. The earthworks are frequently very slight and are often difficult to see – the best time is in the early morning or late evening when the sun is low and the shadows enhance the slight undulations in the ground. Many of the medieval fields contain ridge and furrow and also contain important information concerning the character and extent of arable cultivation at this time.

The fields around the settlements can be grouped into two broad categories: the infield and outfield. The infield immediately surrounded the farm and was used intensively for arable purposes. The outfield generally lay at a further distance and was used occasionally for arable but more often for grazing. Each farm had further grazing rights

47 *Most of the medieval burgage plots leading from the houses in South Zeal still survive and neatly demonstrate the antiquity of this settlement. (Photograph Frances Griffith, Devon County Council: copyright reserved.)*

48 *The extensive field-system at Challacombe consists of a series of lynchets and banks denoting the individual long and narrow fields. (Photograph Frances Griffith, Devon County Council: copyright reserved.)*

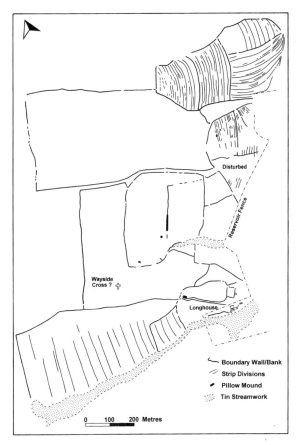

Disturbed

Reservoir Fence

Wayside
Cross ? ✝

Longhouse

⌒ Boundary Wall/Bank
⫽ Strip Divisions
● Pillow Mound
⣿ Tin Streamwork

0   100   200 Metres

49 *The medieval field-system on Holne Moor overlies an earlier co-axial one, evolved through time, and includes stripfields and larger irregular-shaped fields. (After Fleming and Ralph 1982 and Butler 1993.)*

available on the common (unenclosed moorland) which lay beyond the outfield. Grazing of the commons was not limited to those who lived on the moor. Throughout the medieval period, most Devonshire inhabitants had the right to graze animals on the Dartmoor Commons. This activity must have had an impact on the landscape, including the establishment of drove-roads and the building of large numbers of small rectangular buildings, known as sheilings or transhumance huts. These were the seasonal shelters of herdsmen. Similar structures were built and used by peat-cutters, tinners and foresters minding the young deer calves, and this often causes confusion regarding their purpose. In some instances, long-abandoned round houses appear to have been

re-occupied, as witnessed at Holne Moor where a shelter was found built into House F (see **7**). Dating of these structures from field evidence alone is also very difficult and many of those identified might equally belong to other periods.

Control and administration of the earlier medieval landscape was exercised by the Church and State through the feudal system and this has certainly influenced the way in which the landscape was occupied and exploited. The settlements and their fields were laid out following legal and traditional constraints which may only occasionally be ascertained from the documents. The more important centres of medieval power were centred not on the moorland but on its fringes. Here the aristocracy built castles and, later, manor houses from which they controlled their substantial blocks of land on the moor itself. The largest of these estates belonged to the crown, was granted to the Duchy of Cornwall in the early part of the fourteenth century, and was administered through agents based at Lydford Castle. There are four castles (Okehampton, Hembury and two at Lydford) all situated off the high moorland, each of which at one time controlled large areas both on and off Dartmoor. The castles vary in size and character but should never be viewed in isolation, for it must always be remembered that as well as the obvious defensive purpose, they also served as administrative centres thereby affecting the character of their spheres of influence (**50**). The second group of major landowners were the religious houses. These controlled vast tracts of land much of which was used for grazing their large flocks of sheep. Only the abbey at Buckfast survives within Dartmoor, the present edifice being a modern rebuild, but two others – at Tavistock and Buckland – situated on the fringes certainly influenced land-use during the medieval period.

50 *The castles at Lydford and Okehampton. Both masonry castles consist of motte, keep and bailey, though only the one at Okehampton has stone buildings within the bailey. (After Addyman 1966, Higham et al. 1982 and Saunders 1980.)*

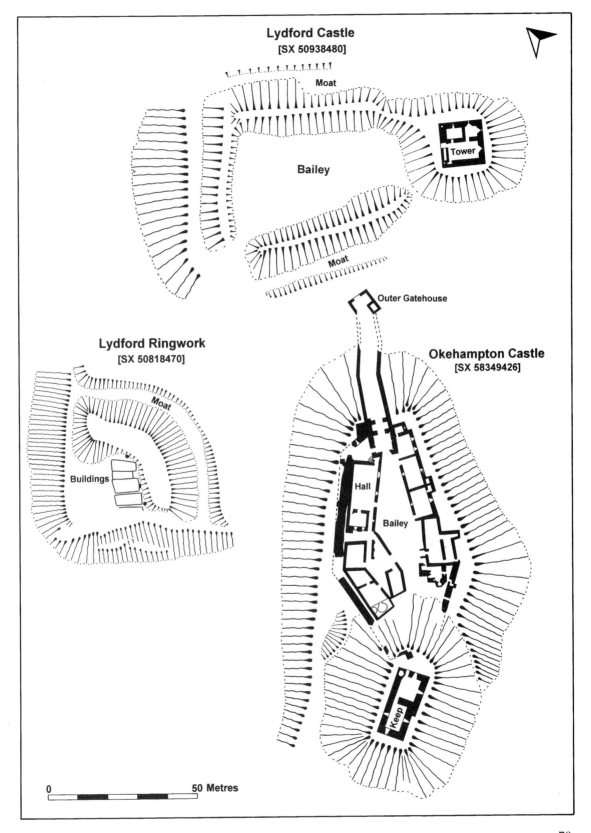

Lydford Castle
[SX 50938480]

Moat

Bailey

Tower

Moat

Outer Gatehouse

Lydford Ringwork
[SX 50818470]

Okehampton Castle
[SX 58349426]

Moat

Buildings

Hall

Bailey

Keep

0   50 Metres

Buckfast Abbey owned several manors including Brent, a large number of bartons (demesne farms) including Pridhamsleigh, grazed sheep on Buckfast Moor and, at the time of the dissolution in 1539, had an annual income amounting to £486. On Dean Moor, a small settlement excavated by Fox is considered to have been a seasonal pastoral establishment called a grange, run by a lay brother of the abbey. At the dissolution, the abbey's lands were sold off and the abbey itself passed to Sir Thomas Dennis who stripped the buildings. During subsequent years the ruins of Buckfast Abbey were extensively quarried for building material, culminating in 1806 when many of the remaining walls were removed to make way for a house and woollen mill. The destruction, fortunately, was not total and among the visible survivals from the medieval period are the gatehouse, guesthouse, various domestic buildings, farmhouse, tithe barn and the foundations, surfaces and features associated with the buildings robbed to ground level.

Religion

In terms of everyday life in the medieval period, the Church had a colossal impact. It administered the rites of passage, formed a focus for social and spiritual interaction, provided a last resting place for the dead and provided the communities with literate clergy at a time of general illiteracy. It comes as no surprise, therefore, to learn of the wealth of contemporary documentary evidence relating to religious activity as a whole. The physical landscape evidence – the stone crosses, churches, churchyards, holy wells and chapels – constitute the medieval equivalent of the prehistoric ritual monuments, but here we have the advantage of written evidence to fill in the blanks regarding ceremonial and cultural influences.

Stone crosses are the most common religious monuments and fall into two main categories: the wayside cross and village or churchyard cross. Of these, wayside crosses are the most numerous. Around 78 still survive, although 111 are known from documentary sources. The crosses had a dual function: they served primarily as way-markers but were also used in a similar way to parish churches and shrines, as places to pray and re-affirm one's Christianity. The location of the crosses has been used to ascertain the routes of medieval trackways, some of which may have been established to link places of religious significance (**51**). Two separate routes, colloquially referred to as the Abbot's Way and Monk's Path, are believed to have linked the three abbeys of Buckfast, Buckland and Tavistock. Both routes are punctuated by crosses. Four religious houses each had varying secular interests on the moor and a number of trackways indicated by crosses illustrate the routes across their estates which were probably utilized at this time.

Several wayside crosses mark routes not directly associated with religious houses, and these indicate established medieval trackways, which might otherwise be unknown. One well-known track, the Lichway, led from settlements around Bellever to Lydford, and, as its name suggests, was used to convey the dead to their final resting places. Surprisingly, this was not marked with crosses, but documentary evidence attests to its use before 1260. Doubtless, other unmarked routes also existed, but these have been lost forever.

Village and churchyard crosses are confined to the larger settlements, generally on the periphery of the moor. Although only hamlets, the presence of the parish church bestowed a greater importance upon them. Village crosses always lie in the parish settlement, but not necessarily in close

51 Marchant's Cross: a wayside cross standing at the junction of several tracks. (Author.)

proximity to the church. Some were probably preaching stations, which pre-dated the churches and latterly became the secular centre of the parish. Churchyard crosses are often situated immediately adjacent to the south door of the church, and are thought to have been erected to sanctify the church enclosure. However, some crosses now located in churchyards were brought in deliberately, so that they might slumber in sanctuary and thus avoid an otherwise ignominious fate. Examples include Manaton, where a nearby cross was placed in an original churchyard socket stone, and Holne where a cross marks the grave of a former vicar. Those less fortunate crosses suffered mutilation, burial or destruction during the Reformation, while others were unceremoniously uprooted and variously deployed as gateposts, garden ornaments and building stones.

The parish churches of Dartmoor with their tall towers and prominent locations have always been dramatic landmarks. Many are larger and more elaborate than expected, the result of certain churches being patronized by wealthy wool merchants and tinners (**Table 4**). The interiors have had mixed fortunes. Many were completely altered during the Reformation, and Restoration,

52 This aspect of the church at Throwleigh highlights its fine Norman doorway, the churchyard cross, Tudor lychgate and in the background the Church House. (Author.)

and later the Victorians renovated them with a resurgence of religious fervour. All the churches have undergone constant change, adaptation and restoration through time, so must be seen as reflecting the dynamic equilibrium of important changes reflected in the various communities which they represent (**52**).

At least twenty-six medieval chapels are known on Dartmoor. Some formed the basis for later churches and were either incorporated into them or demolished to make way for new buildings. Classic examples are Buckfast where a twelfth-century chapel survives beneath the abbey itself, and Sticklepath where a ruinous cob building of *c.* 1180 was replaced by the later church of St Mary's in 1875. Others known as Chapels of Ease served as places of worship supplemental to the parish church. Documentary evidence alone records a site in Moretonhampstead and another at Great Weeke, Chagford. Other chapels belonged to houses and estates. At the manor of Brimley, in Bovey Tracey, traces of the chapel were discovered

Table 4

MAJOR FEATURES AND BUILDING ACTIVITY ASSOCIATED WITH DARTMOOR CHURCHES

NAME	SAXON	NORMAN	C12	C13	C14	C15	C16	C17	C18	C19	C20	NOTES
Ashburton						B				D		Window recess seating. WR. RB. Cruciform.
Belstone		F, P				B					S	WR
Brentor			B	R	R	R						One of smallest in country
Bridford					B	R	S					WR. Tudor bench ends and stalls. Medieval glass.
Buckfastleigh		F		B						D		Porch. Stocks. HWS. Only spire on Dartmoor.
Buckland-in-the-moor			B, F			R						WR. Painted rood screen.
Chagford				B		R						RB. Porch.
Christow		F				B				D		Tudor bench ends.
Cornwood			B			R		R				
Dean Prior		F				B				D		
Drewsteignton						B	R	R		D		
Dunsford					B	R				D		
Gidleigh				B		R	R, S	R		D		Medieval glass.
Hardford						B	R	R				WR. RB.
Hennock				F	B	R, S				D		Medieval glass.
Holne				B	R		S					WR. RB.
Ilsington					B	R	S					Medieval bench ends. WR. RB. Cruciform.
Lustleigh		F		B	R	R	S					C8-C9 memorial stone. Porch. Porch seats. HWS.
Lydford	B, W	F, R				R				D	D	Squint.
Manaton						B, S		R		D	D	Medieval glass.
Mary Tavy						B				D		Porch. WR. Sundial. Stocks.
Meavy			B	R		R	R			D		C13 window. Medieval glass. Norman mouldings.
Moretonhampstead				B		R				D	D	WR. 2 storey porch. Porch seats. HWS.
North Bovey				B		D, S	D					HWS. WR. RB. Tudor bench ends. Porch. Porch
Peter Tavy				B, F	R					D	D	Tudor bench ends.
Sampford Spiney					B		F, R				S	WR. Cruciform.
Sheepstor							B				S	Sundial.
Sourton					B		R, G, F					WR. RB.
South Brent	B	R, F	R		R	R, S						Santuary Ring. Cruciform. Stocks.
South Tawton					B							RB.
South Zeal					B					D		Still classed as chapel.
Throwleigh		B			R	R, S	L					WR. C15 bench ends. Norman door. Tudor lych
Walkhampton					B			R				Slender Porch.
Widecombe-in-the-moor					B	R, S				D		WR. RB. Medieval alter stone. Rood stair.

B = Built
D = Restored
G = Glass
F = Font
HWS = Holy water stoup
L = Lychgate

P = Piscina
R = Rebuilt (or building work continues)
RB = Roof bosses
S = Surviving rood screen
W = Wooden church
WR = Wagon roof

Table 4 *Major features and building activity associated with Dartmoor churches. (Source: Devon SMR.)*

during the building of a leat, and at the manse of Rushford, Chagford, fragments of the chapel fabric were re-used to repair the house and walls. At Filham House, Ugborough, the chapel remains were later remodelled into a folly.

Many chapels have no physical remains still standing, and are known to us only through documentary sources such as dedications, tithe maps and field names. Others survive as ruinous structures in varying stages of dilapidation. A few, such as Fardel chapel, remain standing and, in this particular instance, replete with many original features.

Industrial activity

The moor became a veritable hive of industry during the medieval period, and each activity left its own fingerprint on the landscape. The most dramatic was undoubtedly tinworking, which systematically cut through the landscape like an inept surgeon, leaving it sliced, pock-marked and scarred forever. Doubtless the atmosphere was laced with the pungent smell of charcoal burning. Centuries-old peat was ripped from the uplands. The air resounded to the ringing of stonemen hewing granite slabs. Intricate pillow mounds were constructed to enable intensive husbandry of the highly prized and, at the time, somewhat rare commodity, the rabbit. Elsewhere, millers ground the corn to feed a hungry workforce.

Tinworking

Many of the surviving earthworks and structures relating to the extraction and processing of tin date from the twelfth century until *c.* 1750. Contemporary documentary sources confirm that Dartmoor was a significant producer of tin during this time. At least 835 tinworks are known from these documents and there are also references to the processing sites where ore was treated and transformed into metal, as well as valuable information concerning the techniques employed by the tinners. Administrative documents give details of the legal framework, disputes and output.

The surviving archaeological remains belong to three main categories of site. The first are known collectively as tinworks and these relate to

prospecting and extraction. Many hundreds of hectares of tinworks survive. The second group consists of buildings used by tinners as shelters and storage sheds, and these are often situated immediately next to or even within the tinworks. The third comprises buildings and structures relating to the processing of the ore and these are collectively known as tin mills and include stamping, crazing and blowing mills.

Prospecting was necessary to establish the location, character, quality and extent of tin deposits and lodes before extraction could commence. The most common type of prospecting earthworks to survive are pits, small rectangular hollows with associated crescent-shaped banks. These often occur in lines at right angles to any anticipated lode or deposit. Most tinworks have these 'failed' prospecting pits within their vicinity. The second type of prospecting earthwork are trenches cut across the anticipated line of a lode or deposit. These are much less common and in some instances, such as at Hart Tor, appear to have been excavated with the aid of flowing water to remove much of the overburden in a manner similar to the hushes employed in the lead industry.

On Dartmoor, streamworks are by far the most numerous and extensive type of tinwork and they are found in most valley bottoms and on many hillsides (**53**). Streamworks exploited tin which had been detached from the parent lode and subjected to varying amounts of weathering and transport before coming to rest in deposits known as the tin ground. The tinners extracted the tin using water to wash away the lighter associated clays and sands while leaving behind the heavier cassiterite (tin ore) and any large rocks (**colour plate 9**). The velocity of the water within the work area ('tye') needed to be controlled very carefully. If it flowed too fast, valuable tin would be lost. If it was too sluggish, separation would not occur. To achieve the optimum velocity the tinners either altered the volume of water and/or the gradient of the tye. The deposits on the up-slope side of the work area were removed and thrown into the tye, through which a constant flow of water was channelled. This material was then agitated to

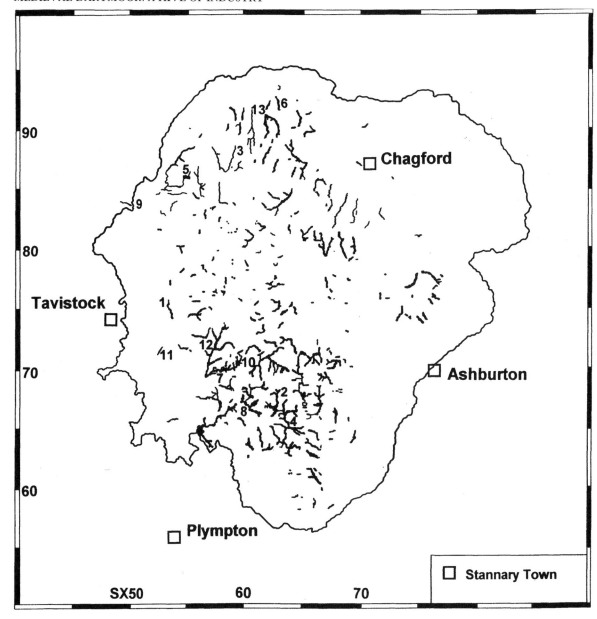

53 *The impact of streamworking on Dartmoor's landscape can be easily understood from this distribution map. The tin deposits lying in most valleys and on many hillsides have been exploited by streamworks and these distinctive earthworks add much to the character of the area.*

1 Beckamoor Combe; 2 Blacklane Brook; 3 Brim Brook; 4 Erme Valley; 5 Great Links Tor; 6 Ivy Tor Water; 7 Keaglesborough; 8 Langcombe; 9 Lydford Woods; 10 Newleycombe Valley; 11 Sampford Wood; 12 Stanlake; 13 Taw River. (Devon SMR.)

release the clays and silts which were carried in suspension downstream, leaving behind the heavier tin, gravels and rocks. The waste gravel and rocks were removed by hand and used to construct a series of fresh lower edges to maintain a constant tye width as work progressed. The result is a series of parallel spoil heaps, which indicate the character and development of each streamwork (**54**). The tin-rich material removed from the tye was transported elsewhere for further processing. At Lydford Woods this secondary dressing was carried out on top of newly abandoned dumps, with the waste being deposited into disused tyes.

There are two main types of streamwork. First, alluvial streamworks are found in valley bottoms and exploited tin located in the alluvium. As work progressed upstream, the earlier banks and features produced were often obliterated beneath the waste deposits from streamworks higher up the valley. Second, eluvial streamworks exploited the tin ground in shallow valleys on the hillsides and are therefore generally situated on steeper slopes. Water was brought to them via a system of artificial channels or leats. Field evidence for such leats is commonplace, and they can be traced for miles running along the contours of many hillsides. Their construction was clearly a major and complex undertaking. Water was stored in reservoirs near to the streamworks, and these vary considerably in size and shape. Compared with the valley bottoms, the quantities of water available on the higher slopes were obviously smaller and less reliable.

With regard to mining, the three different ways of exploiting lode tin are lode-back pit, openwork and shaft. Together these tinworks are collectively known as 'mines' because the cassiterite had to be mined from the ground. Where the lode outcrops, lode-back pits survive in the field as lines of pits

54 *The well-preserved spoil dumps of this streamwork on the upper reaches of the Ivy Tor Water (or Ladybrook) illustrate the systematic manner in which the tin ground was exploited. Leading from the bottom right of the photograph towards the streamwork is a leat which carried water to at least two V-shaped reservoirs. The dark circles on the bottom left are the remains of prehistoric round houses. (RCHME: Crown Copyright: SX 6391/4.)*

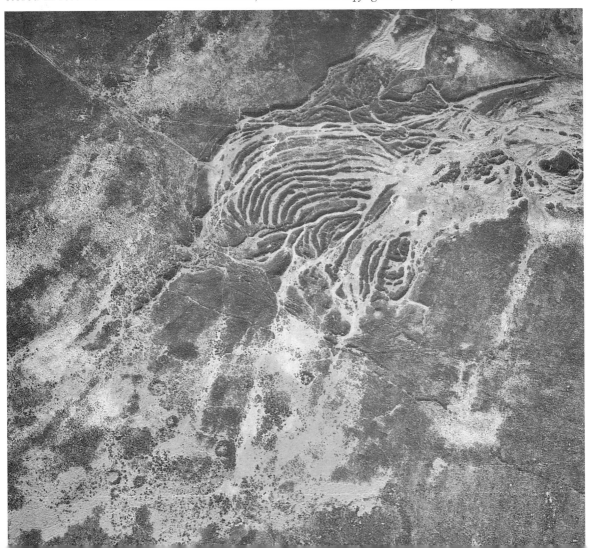

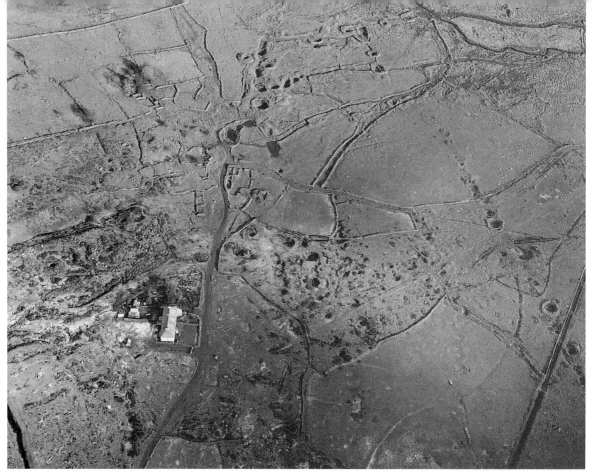

each associated with a spoil dump. They can be distinguished from prospecting pits by their size. They are often over 3m (10ft) deep and 5m (16ft 5in) across. They are usually situated close together, the spoil from one spilling partially into its nearest neighbour (55). These pits allowed access to the upper part of the lode which was then mined until either the ore became too poor in quality to be worth raising, or the pit became flooded. These pits may have been connected to each other by a series of underground tunnels. This type of mine required little capital investment and enabled the accessible part of the lode to be exploited. For these reasons, examples of this type of mine were probably among the earliest. A large number of lodes were exploited using this type of mine, and particularly good examples can be seen within the Newleycombe Valley and at Eylesbarrow.

The second type of mine, the openwork, consists of a relatively deep elongated gully or quarry. At least 300 examples of this type of tinwork are

55 *The distinctive lines of lode-back pits at Whiteworks betray the position of the lodes that were being exploited. (Photograph Frances Griffith, Devon County Council: copyright reserved.)*

thought to survive (56). Openworks were known as 'beams' in the contemporary literature and they were formed by opencast quarrying along the upper length of the lode. Some probably started as lode-back pit workings, while at others, deposits lying above the lode may have been streamed before mining commenced. In some of these circumstances the earlier tinworks may have been completely destroyed by the openwork, though there are many examples where the lode-back workings survive in the area beyond the openwork, and others where lode-back pits survive within the bottom of the openwork. At Down Tor, for example, a single lode has been exploited by alluvial and eluvial streamworking, lode-back pits and openworks (57). Many openworks are served by leats and reservoirs, although it is unclear why

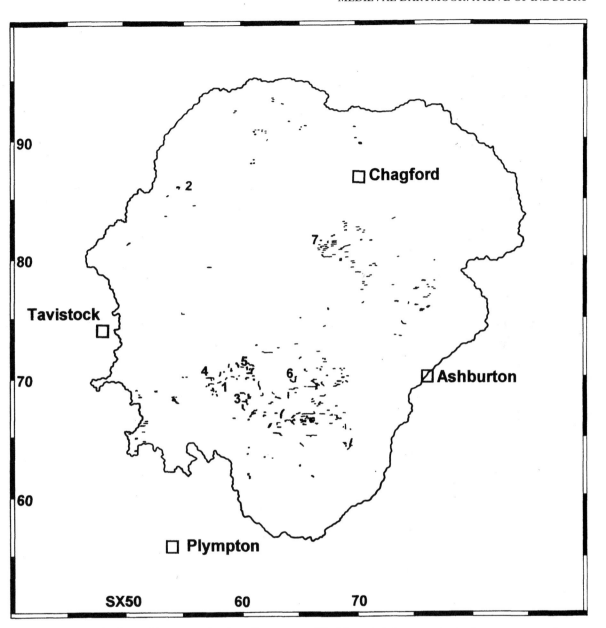

water was required at this type of mine. It may have been for the removal of overburden, sluicing away waste material, fire-setting, earlier stream-working and/or water-powered machinery.

The third type of mine is the shaft, where deep pits were cut through the rock to gain access to deep parts of the lode, inaccessible to surface working. In most instances the shaft was cut to intercept the lode at depth and, in instances where the lode has also been exploited by lode-back pits or openworks, the shafts exploiting the same lode

56 Many tin lodes were mined using opencast quarries called openworks or beams. The distribution map of these features shows that openworks were largely confined to two discrete areas. It is in these areas that evidence for early mines should be sought.

1 Down Tor; 2 Great Links Tor; 3 Eylesbarrow; 4 Keaglesborough; 5 Newleycombe Valley; 6 Skir Gut; 7 Vitifer. (Source: Devon SMR.)

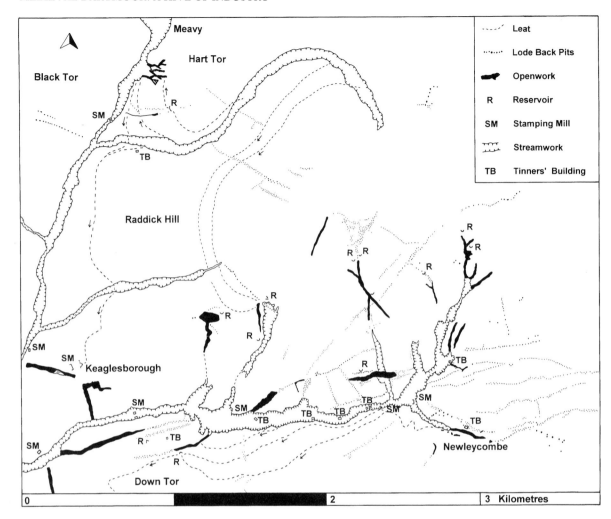

57 A complex array of earthworks record the history of tin exploitation in the Meavy and Newleycombe valleys. The valley bottoms have been streamed, and the lodes have been mined using openworks, lode-back pits and shafts. A system of leats supplied water for the tinworks, mills and dressing floors and scattered throughout the area are the buildings in which the tinners sheltered from inclement weather. Together, these earthworks provide a glimpse of the impact of the industry on the landscape.
(After RAF/CPE/UK/1890 10 DEC 46 F20'
MULTI(4) 58 SQDN. 2360, 2361 & 2362;
and Newman, 1987.)

are therefore generally found at some distance from the earlier workings. By a general rule of thumb, the further the shaft is from the lode outcrop, the deeper it is. Shaft mining is carried out at considerable depth, and the archaeologist faces a 'tip of the iceberg' situation, since surface evidence tends to be restricted to the shaft, spoil dumps, and adit, while clearly much more remains beneath the ground. On Dartmoor, most surviving examples of this type of tinwork probably belong to the period after 1750.

Mining is generally both more difficult and more expensive than tin streaming, and logically only became sensible once the more accessible tin deposits in the valleys had been exhausted. This is probably an over-simplification, but in general terms there does appear to be sound archaeological evidence to support this contention. At Skir Gut and in the Newleycombe Valley, earlier streamworks have been cut through by large openworks, and waste material from another openwork at the upper end of the Newleycombe Valley forms a dump overlying earlier stream-working earthworks. On the lower slopes of Great Links Tor several openworks clearly lead into the side of the hill from the earlier streamworks.

Associated with most tinworks are small rectangular buildings which have been interpreted as shelters. They vary considerably in size, but on average have internal dimensions of 4.84m (15ft 11in) long by 2.7m (8ft 10in) wide. They are defined by a crude dry-stone wall often with a surviving doorway. Some have a fireplace and there may be a cupboard (**58**). Shelters are sometimes built within earlier prehistoric round houses. Most lie within the tinworks and only survive where reworking has not obliterated them. A large number of earlier shelters were probably destroyed in this way. Another form of structure associated with tinworks is the cache. These are very small chambers often composed of dry-stone walling attached to a rock outcrop or earlier feature such as a wall, while others are dug into earlier spoil dumps. They are often circular or oval and are only big enough to hold tools or perhaps black tin (a concentrate of the cassiterite). At least 205 shelters and 40 caches are known to date, although others no doubt await discovery.

The tin ore from the tinworks needed to be processed in order to transform the cassiterite into the metal. Much of the tin collected from streamworks had already been separated from any associated waste (or gangue) material by the streaming process and was already in the form known as black tin. This material would have been taken directly to a blowing mill, where it may have received a final washing prior to smelting. Larger rocks containing cassiterite found during streamworking, together with the ore quarried from the mines, would have been taken first to a stamping mill to be crushed and dressed before being smelted (**59**). Crushing was necessary to release the cassiterite from the gangue minerals with which it was associated. This was achieved by using heavy iron-shod stamps powered by a waterwheel. The stamps, raised by the

58 *This small building in which the tinners sheltered from inclement weather lies within the streamwork at the upper end of Beckamoor Combe. The ranging rod stands with the doorway and the rectangular lintelled recess behind is a fireplace. (Author.)*

rotating axle fell under gravity onto the ore, crushing it between the stamp's head and a hard rock called the mortar stone, on which the ore had been placed. There were two different types of stamping machinery. The first, known as dry stamps, involved the crushing of the ore without water being used to aid the process. This type of machinery appears to have been used through much of the medieval period until the introduction of wet stamping in the sixteenth century. Wet stamping involved using a constant flow of water to carry the tin crushed by the stamps through a fine grate into a channel, to be carried in suspension to a settling pit from where it could be easily collected for dressing.

The archaeological evidence relating to stamping is abundant. At least sixty mills with surviving structural evidence are known to survive (**60**). Stamping mills are very distinctive structures consisting of a rectangular building with an associated wheelpit defined by dry-stone walls, often terraced into the hillslope and containing one or more mortar stones. The continual pounding of the stamps on these stones resulted in the formation of distinctive small saucer-shaped hollows. Some of these stones were turned over several times to allow fresh stone-faces to be exposed to

STAMPING MILLS

**NORSWORTHY
(LEFT BANK)**
[SX 56786958]

LOWER HARTOR
[SX 60486743]

**BLACK TOR FALLS
(RIGHT BANK)**
[SX 57487162]

**BLACK TOR FALLS
(LEFT BANK)**
[SX 57497161]

**IVY TOR WATER
(OR LADYBROOK)**
[SX 62859175]

OUTCOMBE
[SX 58016860]

FISH LAKE FOOT
[SX 64906834]

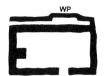

COLESMILLS
[SX 59376676]

**NORSWORTHY
(RIGHT BANK)**
[SX 56746954]

LEFT LAKE
[SX 64006337]

HOOK LAKE
[SX 63936509]

WEEK FORD (UPPER)
[SX 66187232]

BLOWING MILLS

MIDDLE MERRIVALE
[SX 55277624]

LOWER MERRIVALE
[SX 55277535]

AVON
[SX 67226553]

TAW
[SX 62059197]

UPPER MERRIVALE
[SX 55187665]

TEIGNHEAD FARM
[SX 63778426]

GOBBETT
[SX 64537280]

WEEK FORD (LOWER)
[SX 66197234]

0   10   20   30   40 **Metres**

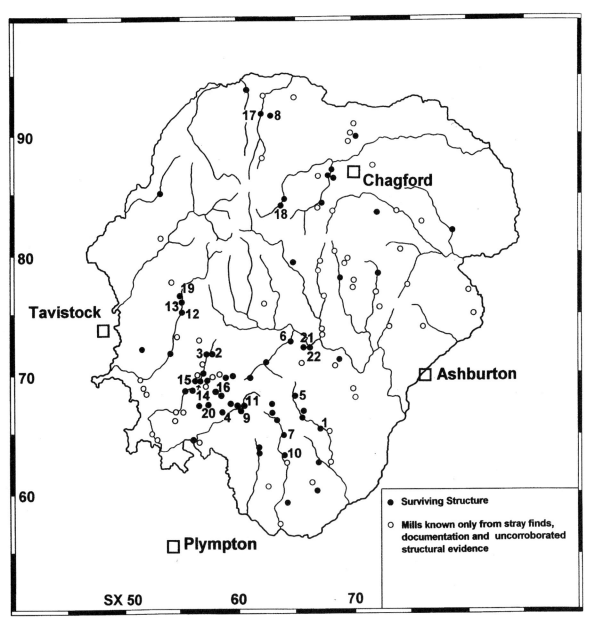

59 *The stamping mills in which the tin ore was crushed are generally smaller than the blowing (smelting) mills. The reason for this would appear to be that blowing mills also often housed stamping machinery to crush slag for reprocessing. Size may be an important criterion in establishing the identity of a mill since the presence or absence of mortar/mould stones cannot always be relied on to positively identify the type of mill. WP = wheelpit. (Gerrard, 1994.)*

60 *The largest number of surviving pre-1750 mill buildings lie in an area containing large numbers of openworks and lode-back pits. It may therefore be assumed that these features are contemporary. 1 Avon; 2 Black Tor Falls (left bank); 3 Black Tor Falls (right bank); 4 Colesmills; 5 Fish Lake Foot; 6 Gobbett; 7 Hook Lake; 8 Ivy Tor Water; 9 Langcombe; 10 Left Lake; 11 Lower Hartor; 12 Lower Merrivale; 13 Middle Merrivale; 14 Norsworthy (left bank); 15 Norsworthy (right bank); 16 Outcombe; 17 Taw; 18 Teignhead Farm; 19 Upper Merrivale; 20 Yellowmead; 21 Week Ford (lower); 22 Week Ford (upper). (Source: Devon SMR.)*

the pounding action; examples of stones re-used in this way have been found at a number of sites including Norsworthy (Left Bank) and Week Ford. However, sometimes the stone selected was not strong enough for the task, or misuse of the machinery caused the stones to crack and break. Positive identification of stamping mills relies on finding at least one mortar stone associated with a mill building. Occasionally, no mortar stones can be found and this makes positive identification of the mill more difficult. To further complicate matters, some mills with visible mortar stones may have primarily been used for smelting tin with the stamps being used to crush slag for reprocessing. Many of the mills lie within or on the edge of alluvial streamworks and survive only because they postdate the last episode of streamworking. Earlier mills in such locations would have been obliterated by later streaming, leaving behind only isolated mortar stones displaced from their original locations. Mortar stones found without any associated mill building probably came from mills destroyed in this way. Some are found in the upper rubble of disused buildings, or built into the walls. These stones had previously been discarded and when the surviving mill was constructed were re-used in the new building. By implication, many surviving mills were rebuilt on at least one occasion during their active life.

Before considering the next stage in the process it is important to mention a second type of mill used for crushing the ore. Crazing mills ground the ore to a fine powder between two circular horizontal stones similar in character to those found in grist mills. This does not appear to have been mandatory in the process. Examples are relatively rare and only three survive at Gobbett, Outcombe and Yellowmead.

During dressing, the lighter gangue minerals were separated from the heavier tin by water flowing through the material from the stamps. As in streamworks the lighter sands, silts and clays were removed in suspension leaving the tin behind. This process was carried out in sloping rectangular- or triangular-shaped boxes called buddles; and to prevent premature sedimentation of the clays in

particular, shovels were used to agitate the contents. The skill was to ensure that as little tin as possible was lost and as much as possible of the gangue minerals were removed. In order to achieve this, the material was put through the buddles a number of times. Archaeological evidence for buddles is relatively abundant with clearly defined hollows surviving at a number of tin mills including Ivy Tor Water, Upper Merrivale, Black Tor Falls (right bank), Norsworthy (left bank) and Langcombe. At sites with no surface evidence, buddles probably survive as buried features.

The end-product of the crushing and dressing process was black tin similar in character to that from the streamworks. This material was taken to the blowing mill to be smelted. At the blowing mill the tin may have been washed a final time before being put into the furnace together with charcoal (**61**). To smelt tin the temperature within the furnace had to reach 1150°C. This was achieved by blowing air through the furnace using water-powered bellows. Once the tin had become molten, it flowed from the furnace into a float and was ladled into a bevelled rectangular trough called a mouldstone, in which it cooled to form an ingot of white tin. Blowing mills survive in the field as large rectangular dry-stone buildings served by one or more leats and are characterized by the presence of granite blocks with moulds cut into them – the mouldstones – and on occasion by the square or rectangular stone-built base of the furnace itself.

Contemporary documentation indicates that at least 136 kilograms (300lb) of white tin could be produced from a furnace during a twelve-hour period. The ingots of tin were taken to the nearest stannary town for payment of tax before being sold to the merchants attending the biannual tin sales.

The immense physical impact of the tin industry on the landscape is beyond doubt. Its rich archaeological legacy confirms the important nature of this activity to the moorland economy. The effects of the industry, however, extended well beyond the moor; the final product was utilized throughout Europe, while closer to home,

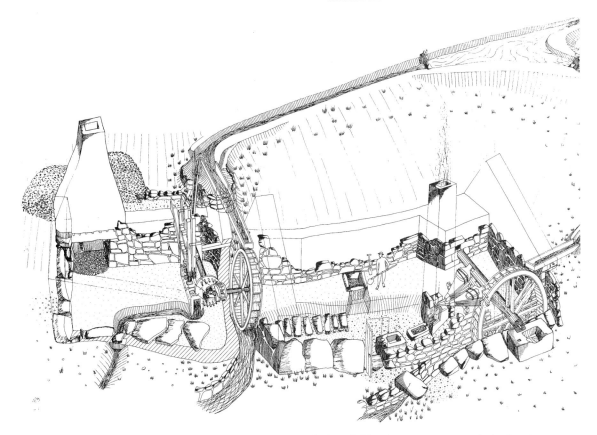

61 *Recent excavations at Upper Merrivale have revealed a complex tin-processing site. In its final phase of use the tin ore was crushed in the mill on the left before being taken to the blowing mill for smelting. Mills sometimes occur in pairs but the two at Merrivale are untypically connected and the picture at other sites must have been significantly different to the one illustrated here. (Robert Waterhouse: copyright reserved.)*

the wastes which were constantly being discharged into the streams must have caused widespread environmental damage to the wildlife in the rivers and estuaries.

Peat cutting and peat charcoal-burning

Peat played an important role in Dartmoor's medieval economy. It is impossible to quantify how much was extracted but it is clear that it was a convenient source of fuel for both domestic use and the tin-blowing mills. As early as 1201 the first charter of the stannaries confirms the ancient custom of 'digging tin and turves for smelting at all times'. Further stannary and duchy documentation throughout the medieval period indicates the importance of peat extraction, and it is known that a charge of 5d per year was levied in the fourteenth century on all peat-cutters who were not holders of ancient tenements. When cut, the turves contain a large volume of water, much of which was removed by drying the material in stages (**colour plate 10**). First, the turves were placed in pairs leaning against each other. Next they were placed into small piles called stooks and finally into larger heaps called ricks. In particularly wet years the peat within the ricks would not dry sufficiently and would be wasted. Examples of ricks which did not dry survive as mounds within peat cutting areas, and sometimes, as at Greena Ball, they have been confused with prehistoric round cairns. Once dried, the peat destined for the blowing mill was slowly burnt in meilers or kilns to produce the charcoal needed for smelting purposes. Peat cut for domestic consumption was dried in the same manner and then carted by pack animals to the moorland settlements, where it was used as a fuel for heating and cooking. The archaeological evidence for peat cutting includes the rectangular pit from which the peat was excavated, the meilers, kilns, peat-cutters shelters and trackways leading from the workings. The rectangular extraction pits are called ties and survive as shallow, flat-bottomed hollows with relatively steep and straight sides. Such remains may be found in most parts of the moor where deep peat deposits are known to exist. Particularly extensive areas of peat cutting are known to survive over large tracts of the northern moor. The areas with the richest and most suitable peat deposits are generally remote from the settlements. Thus, shelters were often built near to the ties in which workers took refuge from inclement weather and some may have been used as temporary accommodation. These buildings are similar in character to those found near tinworks and generally include a one-roomed rectangular dry-stone structure with a fireplace.

Wood charcoal-burning

Wood charcoal was also used for smelting tin and the woodland around the fringes of the moor was exploited for this purpose. The hearths in which the wood was reduced to charcoal were formed by digging a circular pit in which the wood was placed. Earth from the pit and the surrounding area, if necessary, was thrown up over the wood in order to control the amount of oxygen entering the hearth. The wood pile was then fired and burnt ferociously for a short time before being dampened down by the addition of further earth over the remaining inlets. The hearth burnt very slowly for a few days, with the amount of air entering being severely limited. Once firing was complete the charcoal was removed, leaving behind a circular hollow surrounded by a low bank formed from the lower part of the earth capping. These structures are very similar in appearances to prehistoric round houses but can be distinguished by their hollow centres, lack of obvious door, woodland setting and few visible stones in the surrounding bank. A large number of these structures have been found

in three distinct clusters in woodland around the eastern fringes of the moor. The first lies within the Teign Valley between Steps Bridge and Castle Drogo, the second at Holne Chase, and the third in King's Wood, Buckfastleigh. The date of these particular structures is unknown since the industry continued into the early part of the twentieth century. The possibility of some being medieval cannot be discounted.

Rabbit farming

Although this might be considered an agricultural rather than industrial activity, rabbit farming was highly specialized and restricted to a few locations (**62**). The most obvious surviving features are the pillow mounds or buries. These survive as long, flat-topped mounds surrounded by a ditch. The mounds cover interconnecting tunnels which were capped with flat stones or turves, and acted as artificial burrows. Rabbits prized for their meat and fur were deliberately introduced, fed and fenced in. In this way, the warrener was able to control the population.

Leading downslope from some mounds are narrow gullies which have been interpreted as drainage gullies. These gullies sometimes lead into complex and extensive systems of ditches, which often terminate in a vermin trap – and in these circumstances it seems more likely that they represent animal runs. Vermin traps are essentially stone-built funnels which directed the vermin (and rabbits) into a centrally placed, stone box. They became trapped alive when they tripped a strategically placed lever. The warrener regularly checked the traps, killing the vermin and releasing the rabbits necessary to maintain the population. The gullies running into the traps are either X-shaped, an example being found immediately below the summit rocks at Legis Tor; or V-shaped, like one on the western slopes of Trowlesworthy. Sometimes prehistoric walling or tinners' spoil dumps have been re-used in these features.

The warrens are often defined by rabbit-proof walls designed to keep the rodents in. At Legis Tor a series of contemporary enclosures defined by a

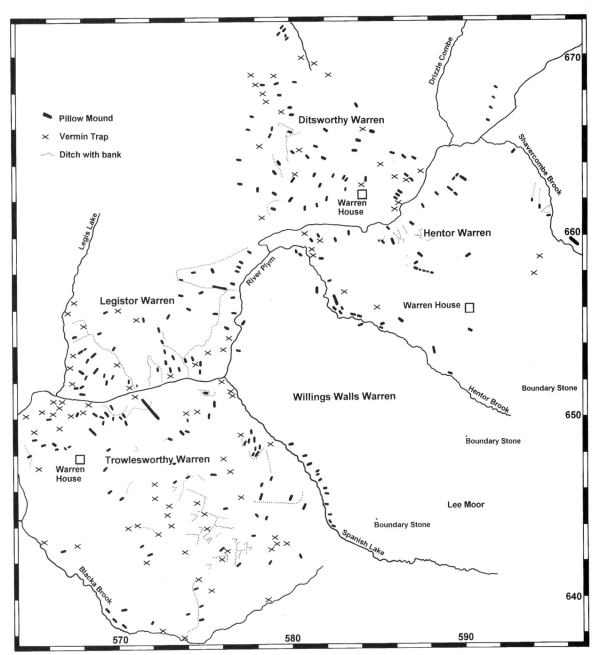

62 *The pillow mounds, vermin traps, animal runs and enclosures associated with five warrens survive within the Upper Plym Valley. Many of these features probably belong to post-medieval rabbit exploitation, but some are certainly of medieval origin. (Source: Devon SMR and Mercer, 1986.)*

ditch and bank are visible within the warren and probably reflect sophisticated husbandry techniques (**63**). Rabbits were trapped in nets placed over the burrows or spread over large areas of the warren, and some must have also been caught in the vermin traps. Warreners' houses are also known, but all are post-medieval, although they may have been rebuilt on the sites of medieval ones. The warrens in the Upper Plym Valley seem to have been located to supply large settlements like Plymouth and Tavistock, while some may have served tinners and other industrial workers.

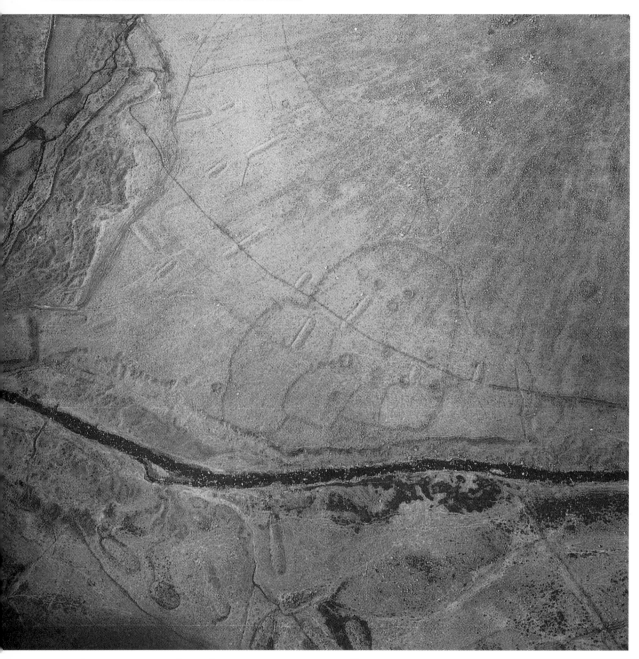

63 *The pillow mounds at Legis Tor lie within and around a partially enclosed prehistoric settlement which includes a good example of an agglomerated enclosure. The narrow gully leading from top to bottom just right of this enclosure is probably an artificially excavated animal run in which vermin and rabbits were trapped. The earthworks lying adjacent to the rivers are those formed by streamworking. (RCHME: Crown Copyright: SX5765/4.)*

Stone quarrying

The character and extent of granite quarrying during the medieval period is not known. Farm buildings, clapper bridges (**64**) and walls were generally built from unworked stone, presumably cleared from the fields or collected from the surface. Some stone was worked, for example into crosses, troughs, mould stones, mill stones and used for ecclesiastical buildings (see **52**). Given the

64 *The earlier clapper bridge (foreground) was replaced by the later bridge when the turnpike road was built. (Author.)*

abundant quantities of surface stone available to the medieval stoneworker it seems unlikely that deep quarrying started at this time. Large boulders lying at the surface were probably selected and cut in situ using the wedge-and-groove technique. This method involved cutting a series of narrow rectangular holes into which wedges were then forced until the rock split. Large numbers of stones cut in this manner survive and can be identified by a series of shallow rectangular hollows along the upper edge of the remaining stone. In some instances the task was never completed and a line of small rectangular hollows cut into the face of the rock can be seen. It is generally accepted that this method for cutting stone ceased around 1800.

Corn milling

The milling of grain from demesne land was strictly controlled by the lord of the manor in whose mills it had to be ground. This may in part explain why most of the corn mills were situated on the lower ground around the periphery of the moor and continued in use until recently.

6

The post-medieval landscape

A dramatic increase in the quantity and quality of documentation combined with a burgeoning variety of site types means that our understanding of the history of this period (AD 1500 onwards) is greater than for any other. Perhaps, because of this, the archaeological legacy of this period has been less well-studied. There are of course exceptions, with mining in particular being the subject of much research. One would perhaps anticipate that, by virtue of its position at the end of a long chronological development, the post-medieval landscape would be the best preserved and most complete. This is the case, but much of the earlier post-medieval evidence has been altered, damaged or destroyed by intensive activity in recent years. So even for this period one is dealing with only partial evidence. The only landscape which is complete is that of today.

Settlement

A much greater diversity of settlement types serving a variety of different purposes exist within this period (**65**). Many of the earlier medieval farmsteads continued in occupation, and while some were enlarged during the sixteenth and seventeenth centuries others were abandoned (**66**). Most notably twenty-four farmsteads and dwellings were cleared to make way for the new Burrator Reservoir. New farms were also established and some of these were also deserted after only a relatively short period. Many of the new farms were established between the ends of the eighteenth and nineteenth centuries and are of two main types.

The first were the large concerns financed by 'improvers' of considerable wealth such as Thomas Tyrwhitt who established Tor Royal in 1785 and spent large quantities of money enclosing, draining and fertilizing the land. Other similar ventures included those at Prince Hall, the Prison Farm and Bear Down. The second type of new farm was the smallholding, where small areas of previously unenclosed land were leased to agricultural and industrial workers. These ventures were not backed by capital and instead relied largely on the leasee's own endeavours. The result was often failure, since this type of agricultural enterprise was not suited to the conditions which the moor offered. Many examples of these failed deserted farmsteads survive. Some, such as those at Merrivale and Shavercombe Foot, do not appear to have gone beyond establishing the house and garden plot. At others, the end was longer in coming, and at Mis Tor some of the smallholdings remained in occupation until the early part of the twentieth century. In total approximately 6070 hectares (15,000 acres) were enclosed and brought into cultivation during this period and the impact on the landscape of the area, particularly between Princetown and Postbridge, is marked. Substantial granite walls composed of large blocks, rather than the earlier rubble walls, can be seen enclosing extensive areas. Within these areas archaeological features of earlier periods are relatively rare, and it must be assumed that much of the earlier landscape was obliterated at this time. We should be extremely grateful that such enclosures were not

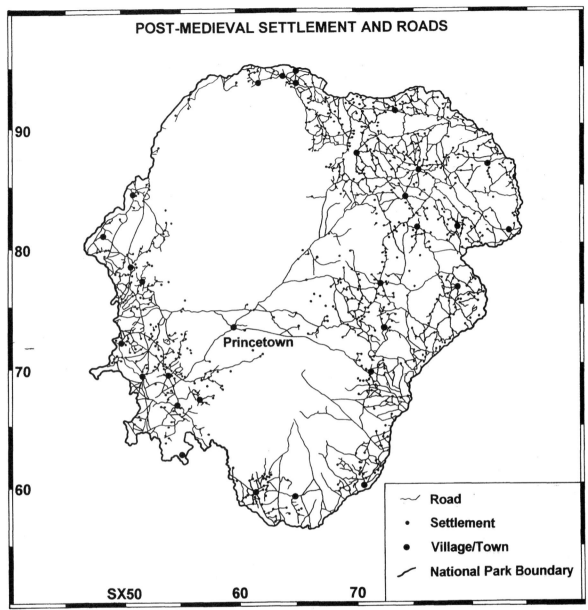

POST-MEDIEVAL SETTLEMENT AND ROADS

Princetown

	Road
•	Settlement
●	Village/Town
	National Park Boundary

SX50   60   70

65 *The post-medieval settlement pattern is similar to the medieval one and many of the roads probably continued in use from the earlier period. (Ordnance Survey one-inch map, 1863.)*

more extensive or else the quality of Dartmoor's earlier archaeology would have been severely compromised.

The most fundamental change in the settlement pattern was the introduction of industrial housing. At several of the mines and quarries, terraces of cottages were built to house the workforce. Housing was built within the environs of the quarries at Merrivale, Foggintor and Haytor, a settlement grew up around the china clay works at Lee Moor, and miners' cottages were erected to serve the tin mine at Whiteworks. At other mines, such as Vitifer, dormitory accommodation was provided.

At Princetown a settlement was established to service the new prison which was completed in 1809. In other locations, public houses, smithies,

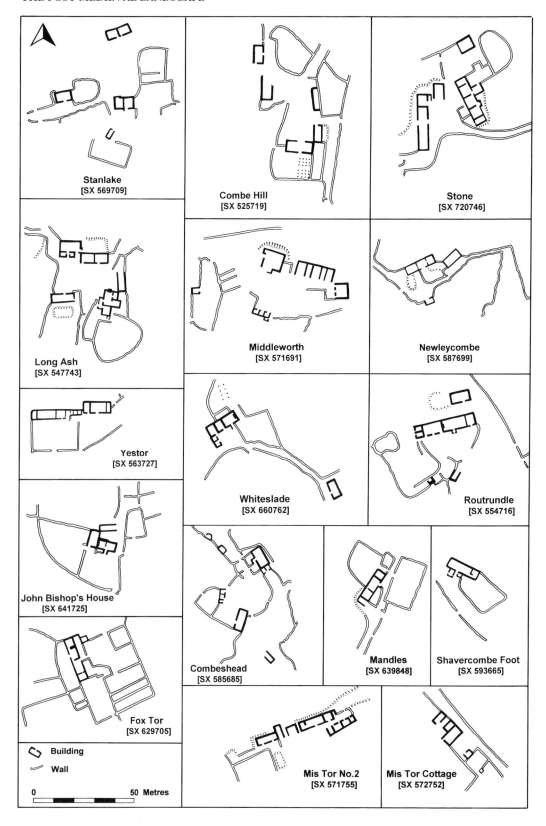

Stanlake
[SX 569709]

Combe Hill
[SX 525719]

Stone
[SX 720746]

Long Ash
[SX 547743]

Middleworth
[SX 571691]

Newleycombe
[SX 587699]

Yestor
[SX 563727]

Whiteslade
[SX 660762]

Routrundle
[SX 554716]

John Bishop's House
[SX 641725]

Combeshead
[SX 585685]

Mandles
[SX 639848]

Shavercombe Foot
[SX 593665]

Fox Tor
[SX 629705]

Mis Tor No.2
[SX 571755]

Mis Tor Cottage
[SX 572752]

Building

Wall

0   50 Metres

66 *This selection of deserted post-medieval farmsteads illustrates the considerable variation in their size and character. Many farms continue in use to this day and these deserted ones are illustrated because they show the character of different types before modern farming practices revolutionized the layout of many farmsteads. (After Haynes.)*

schools and chapels were built to cater for the increased population, much of which was involved in new and expanding industrial concerns.

Most dramatic, however, was the nineteenth-century expansion of the towns around the periphery of the moor. At Buckfastleigh the woollen industry, tanning, engineering, paper manufacturing and corn milling developed at this time. At nearby Ashburton, woollen and corn mills together with a prosperous market meant that between 1801 and 1851 the population rose from 3080 to 3432. Tavistock, lying on the periphery of the moor, probably supplied the labour for many of the industrial concerns on Dartmoor while also serving as centre for a number of foundries and a market. Between 1801 and 1851 its population rose from 3420 to 8147, although following the disastrous collapse in copper mining, emigration was rife and by 1901 the figure had fallen to 5841.

Religion

The details of religious beliefs and practices are well understood for this period and need not be dwelt upon here. It is sufficient to note that although no longer Roman Catholic, the earlier churches continued in use and remained dependent on the resources of each parish for their support. In common with many parts of England a large number of churches were 'restored' during the Victorian period, and in many cases the inevitable result was a loss of interesting earlier features. Most of the surviving tombs and grave markers within and surrounding the churches belong to this period. A number of new churches were built to serve new communities and among these are Princetown (opened in 1814), Yelverton (built between 1910 and 1912) and Postbridge, where a mission chapel constructed in 1868 was consecrated in 1934 by the Bishop of Exeter.

The spread of Nonconformism particularly during the nineteenth century resulted in the construction of a large number of chapels. Nonconformity was especially strong within the towns and among the industrial workers in particular. Thus we find chapels built specifically to serve the clay workers of Lee Moor and Bittaford, and some such as the one at Lettaford within a hamlet to serve agricultural workers, but it was more normal for the chapels to be built within the towns where many of the workers from both factories and moorland industrial ventures lived together. In most towns there was at least one nonconformist chapel and in some, such as South Brent, Ashburton and Moretonhampstead, there were examples representing several denominations.

Communications

Communications, so important to the success of the moorland economy in earlier times, were improved with the building of turnpike roads (see **64**) and, more significantly, the introduction of railways. Many of the ancient trackways continued in use, but remained only suitable for pack-animals.

The railways, together with their cuttings, embankments, bridges and associated buildings were primarily built to carry granite, china clay, peat and passengers. At least fourteen distinct railways are known some of which were used only by horse-drawn trucks. The first railway was opened in 1820 and was constructed to carry granite from the five separate quarries at Haytor to the Stover Canal. This railway, known as the Haytor Granite Tramway, has a rail bed composed of skilfully shaped granite blocks, many of which still survive. Another railway constructed to serve the nineteenth-century granite quarries was the Plymouth and Dartmoor Railway which ran from Princetown to Crabtree Wharf and served quarries on Walkhampton Common including King's Tor, Foggintor, Swelltor and Ingra Tor. Much of this line was later adopted by the Yelverton to Princetown Branch of the Great Western Railway.

Three railroads were constructed to carry commercially cut peat from the moor. The Omen Beam tramroad leading from the upper reaches of the Blackbrook to the prison at Princetown was constructed in 1846 by the British Patent Naphtha Company to carry peat to their gas plant. In the same year a licence was granted for a railroad to carry peat from Red Lake (see **69**) to a naphtha works at Shipley Bridge. The third, which finally went out of use in 1937, went to Rattlebrook from the Great Western Railway at Bridestowe Station. Two railroads were constructed specifically to serve the china-clay industry. The Lee Moor Tramway was built to transport workers and supplies to and from the Lee Moor china-clay pits. The Red Lake railway, surveyed by Worth, served the clay pits at Red Lake (see **69**). The remaining railway lines on Dartmoor were specifically constructed to carry passengers and freight. Among these are the Plympton to Tavistock line, Yelverton to Princetown branch line, two separate lines between Tavistock and Lydford Junction, Lydford Junction to Okehampton, Newton Abbot to Moretonhampstead, and Buckfastleigh to Ashburton. The lines between Tavistock and Lydford Junction were operated independently by the Great Western Railway and Southern Railways and at Lydford there are consequently two stations.

Travel on the high moor was improved by the provision of peat passes, many of which were constructed between 1895 and 1905 by Frank Phillpotts. These consist of passages cut through the turf and embankments built over marshy ground. Phillpotts took care to follow existing natural erosion gullies, so many appear to be features of the natural landscape and are often only detectable by a small granite marker placed at the end of each pass.

Quarrying

Granite has been used as a building material since the Neolithic period, but until the post-medieval period, exploitation was limited to surface stone. Until about AD 1800 granite was split using the wedge-and-groove method. After this time a much more efficient method known as 'feather-and-tare' was adopted. This technique involved cutting a line of 3-inch (7.5cm) deep circular holes using a chisel

or metal bar called a jumper. Metal wedges (called tares), supported by pieces of metal (called feathers), were inserted into each of the holes and hit with a sledgehammer until the rock split along the line of the holes. Evidence for this activity is found throughout the granite areas of the moor where rocks with small circular half-holes around one edge can be seen. A large number of these stones remain visible on the lower slopes of Staple Tor where there is also considerable evidence of the production of granite paving-stones, kerbs and setts for the expanding industrial towns and cities. On the eastern slopes of the tor are at least 100 stone benches, on which the stone was shaped (Paul Rendell, pers. comm.). These 'sett-maker bankers', as they are called, often occur in groups of two or three, and large quantities of granite waste chips are generally found in the immediate vicinity (**67**).

Another form of feature associated with granite extraction are the shallow flat-bottomed linear hollows often found on clitter-strewn slopes (slopes of detached granite boulders). A particularly fine group of these proto-quarries are visible on the southern slopes of Leeden Tor, and they would appear to be the result of surface extraction of detached stone.

Surface stone had many uses, for example as grave stones, memorials, gate and door hangers, millstones, cheese-presses, troughs, manger stones, stone rollers and cider presses. Many of these stones were shaped at source and examples of unfinished or broken examples have been found. At Sourton Tor, close to the earlier stone circle, is the base of a cider mill, while within an enclosure at Merrivale lies an apple-crusher stone (see **10**). The majority of the stone removed from the hillsides was not worked. Instead it was used to build the multitude of buildings and other structures which together provide the durable evidence of life and work at this time. Stone was easily available and was used to construct many of the everyday items which elsewhere would have been made of wood. No list of the many uses to which this building material was put could ever hope to be exhaustive as the ingenuity and tenacity of the local people has provided us with an extraordinarily

67 The sett-makers' bankers on the slopes of Middle Staple Tor were built and used by granite masons producing pavement setts. The worker knelt in front of the banker and chiselled the stone collected from the clitter slopes nearby. Surrounding each banker are the chippings from their work. The curving dry-stone wall at this site would have offered some protection from fierce winds. (Paul Rendell: copyright reserved.)

varied legacy of structures. Obviously, field boundaries, various dwellings, barns and industrial structures dominate the landscape. However, we also find items such as dog kennels, milk churn stands, duck and geesehouses, pigeon nest holes, pigsties, bee boles, rick bases, and boundary markers which are not commonly stone-built elsewhere.

Quarrying is generally considered to have started around 1780 and since this date has made a considerable impact on the appearance of several parts of the moor. The quarries generally include a

68 The granite quarry at Foggintor. The largest finger-shaped dump leading from the quarry partly overlies an earlier field. (Author.)

large sharp-sided pit excavated into the side of a hill accompanied by a series of narrow linear dumps spreading out from the pit, several building platforms, occasionally traces of industrial housing and tramways (**68**). The granite from the quarries was used for many purposes and among the better known final destinations are London Bridge, the British Museum and Nelson's Column. The earliest quarries employed the 'feather-and-tare' technique. This was soon replaced by drills and explosives which considerably speeded up the process. Most of the largest quarries were linked to their markets by railroads, although there is a notable exception at Merrivale where road transport was used to cart the stone to Tavistock. In addition to the large quarries, there are a small number which were excavated for specific projects. Amongst these are the quarry near Burrator Reservoir, from which stone was quarried to build the nearby dam, and that at Rutt near Western Beacon which provided building material for viaducts at Ivybridge, Cornwood and Bittaford.

China clay

The impact of the 160-year-old china-clay industry on the landscape of the south-western part of Dartmoor is considerable. The substantial waste dumps can be seen for miles and the associated pits are immense when compared with those created by other mining and quarrying activities over the centuries. Most of the very large pits and dumps belong to the second half of the twentieth century and are still being exploited. More typical examples of the smaller-scale nineteenth- and early twentieth-century activity can be seen at Red Lake, Left Lake, Knatta Barrow Pool and Wigford Down (**69**). A typical nineteenth-century china-clay work included the pit itself, a conical spoil dump, at least one leat, a drainage adit, buildings, tramways and a channel or pipeline to carry the clay solution to the clay-drying plant, which at many sites was located a considerable distance from the pit. The quarrying process has changed over the years, becoming increasingly mechanized, but in the earliest works the process involved first clearing by hand the overburden to expose the

69 *The china-clay pit at Red Lake showing the pit from which the clay was removed and the conical spoil dump. The parallel lines on the left-hand side of the photograph are earlier disused peat working earthworks. (Photograph Frances Griffith, Devon County Council: copyright reserved.)*

kaolinized granite from which the china clay was to be extracted. A leat was brought to the area and the water dropped onto the deposits which were further broken down using picks and shovel to produce a china-clay slurry. This slurry was then pumped through a previously cut level (horizontal tunnel) and shaft to the surface. It was often washed and de-sanded before being pumped through a pipeline or open channel to the clay-drying plant. It was left in pits to settle out. By the time it reached a consistency where it could be shovelled, it was taken to the 'dry' – a building in which coal-fired kilns completed the drying process. The blocks of clay were then transported by rail to markets both in Britain and abroad. The archaeological evidence for all stages of the process (with the exception of the underground level and shaft) are visible at many locations.

Tinworks

The earthworks and structures associated with several tinworks dating from the latter part of the

eighteenth century survive. Many mines expanded, contracted and were renamed on several occasions, so it is difficult to be precise concerning the total number of mines which produced tin during this period. The nature and character of the surviving evidence is generally very different to that from the earlier period. Most of the ore was extracted using deep shaft mines, with streamworks and openworks being only very rarely employed.

Shaft mines gave access to the parts of the lode which had been inaccessible to earlier tinners. In contrast to the earlier tinworks a number of other structures may be directly associated with shaft mines. Material dug from the shaft had to be raised to the surface and there are a number of devices which were used. Windlasses used a cylinder called a barrel onto which rope attached to a bucket or kibble was wound by the tinners. In horse-whims the rope was lowered and raised by horses or mules pushing against crossbeams attached to a centrally, vertically positioned cylinder onto which the rope was wound. Whim-platforms with or without a central stone in which the cylinder pivoted are found at many sites in Cornwall, but appear to be rare on Dartmoor, although at least one is known from an early nineteenth-century map, another five survive within the Eylesbarrow area, at least two at Whiteworks and a further example at Bachelors Hall Mine. In contrast to Cornwall, very few mines on Dartmoor were served by steam-powered machines which pumped water from the mine and brought up the ore and workers. The best-preserved engine house lies adjacent to Job's Shaft at Wheal Betsy, which was primarily a silver, lead and copper mine (**colour plate 11**). On Dartmoor, most of the mines were water-powered and a more common means of getting power to the shaft for pumping purposes was by the use of flat-rods, driven from a wheel at some distance from the shaft. Upright stones on which these rods moved to-and-fro survive at Eylesbarrow where a wheelpit excavated into the top of a disused shaft provided the power to drive a set of rods. At other sites the flat rods rested on wooden or metal stanchions which have since been removed; all that remains in these instances is a gully cut into the hillside in which the rods ran. Examples of this type of site can be found at Mary Tavy and East Birch Tor Mine.

Within the vicinity of mines from 1750 onwards, a range of buildings and other structures are found (**70**). Each mine tended to have a slightly different range of buildings, depending on the scale of the operation and the minerals being extracted. It is beyond the scope of this book to examine in detail the precise function and layout of these buildings or to consider their

70 At Foxhole mine, circular buddles, a range of buildings, well-preserved leat embankment, wheelpit and tramway survive in close proximity to an earlier tin streamwork. (Author.)

architectural character, but it is perhaps useful to indicate the types of buildings found at these sites. Excluding those structures associated with the dressing of the ore (considered separately below), the structures found on Dartmoor mines include the blacksmith's shop in which tools were repaired and sharpened, the count house or mine office for administration, the dry in which wet clothing was hung, the mine captain's house, miners' cottages, the powder house in which gunpowder for blasting was kept, store rooms for equipment and tin, and tramways for moving the ore and equipment around the surface.

With regard to processing, the stamping and crushing was generally carried out close to the mine and the technique employed at some stamping mills differed only slightly from the earlier methods. Mortar stones were now no longer used. Instead, larger numbers of stamp heads were driven from a single wheel. At some mills, however, considerable improvements were introduced including Californian stamps (with a stamp head which rotated as it hit the ore, thus increasing the efficiency of the stamping process), rock crushers and rotary pulverizers. The archaeological evidence confirms these differences in character and scale. The wheelpits are generally larger and are not associated with the small rectangular buildings of the earlier period. Most sets of stamps appear to have been sited in the open air, although towards the end of the period corrugated iron sheds were sometimes built over the crushing and dressing facilities. The dressing floors are much more obvious and are often defined on three sides by walls enclosing either large rectangular buddles, such as

those at Eylesbarrow, or circular ones such as those found at Foxhole, Hooten Wheals, Wheal Mary Emma and West Vitifer. The introduction of the circular buddle was an important development during this period. The tin was separated from the gangue minerals on a circular shaking and rotating platform over which the crushed ore and water was run. This improvement, together with the use of classifiers, various types of tables and the continued use of rectangular buddles in certain circumstances, greatly improved the efficiency of the dressing process. This made previously uneconomic ores more profitable and must have radically reduced the number of people required to dress a given quantity of black tin.

Much of the black tin produced during this later period was smelted in reverberatory furnaces, although blast (or blowing) furnaces continued to be used. The reverberatory furnaces used coal rather than charcoal as a fuel and although this necessitated further refining of the tin after the smelting process, there were many other advantages including the abandonment of bellows, greater fuel economy, faster smelting times and a more durable furnace. The last smelting works to operate survives at Eylesbarrow where between 1822 and 1831, 276 tons of metallic tin was produced. The walls of this smelting house remain visible together with substantial granite blocks which represent the site of the two furnaces, and from the northern wall of the structure the flue can still be traced leading away from the building. After this smelting house closed, all black tin produced from the mines was sent to furnaces in other parts of the country.

Other mines

In addition to tin, a large variety of other minerals was commercially exploited. In many instances mines produced more than one product. For example, Many Waters Mine produced lead, barytes, cobalt and copper. At Wheal Friendship, arsenic, copper, iron, lead, silver, tungsten, zinc and tin were extracted. For these reasons one has to rely on the documentation to ascertain exactly which minerals were being mined at a particular site. The nature of the surviving structures associated with these ventures varies considerably. At some, only the shaft or opencast quarry is visible, while elsewhere a range of buildings, leats, dressing floors and tramways remain (**71**).

The impact of mining upon the landscape has been considerable both on the surface and beneath it. It forms a crucial part in the history of the moor, both for the tangible evidence which attests to its existence and in the social and economic legacy which it has left behind.

Other industrial activities

A number of other industrial activities helped to model this unique landscape, some having a more profound physical effect than others. These industries are briefly considered here.

Evidence for a few brickworks remains. At Halford Cross, bricks were produced from the eighteenth century until 1914. Woollen processing mills were generally located on the moorland fringe to utilize the plentiful supplies of water. Ashburton, Buckfastleigh and Chagford, especially, had strong connections with the woollen industry. Today, some of the buildings still survive, although they tend to have been converted and re-used.

On the north-western edge of the moor near the Meldon Viaduct a glass factory was established towards the end of the nineteenth century. This took advantage of the locally available granulite, which when quarried and calcined was particularly suitable for glass manufacture. Another unusual industrial enterprise on the north-western side of the moor was an iceworks established at Sourton Tor in 1875. A series of long, rectangular, embanked hollows were cut into the hillside to receive water from a nearby spring and when frozen the ice was broken up and carried to a large insulated underground storage building, from which it was transported during the spring and early summer months. This venture only lasted about eleven years, but the impressive pond earthworks still survive largely intact.

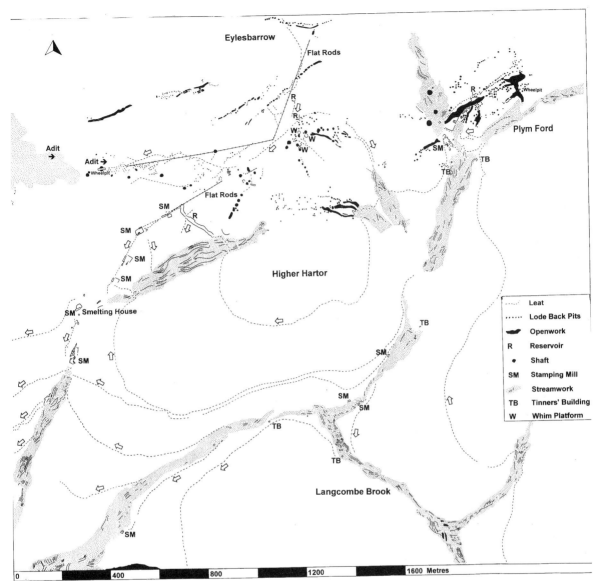

71 *Many of the industrial earthworks and structures within this area relate to the nineteenth-century Eylesbarrow Mine. The tin ore extracted from the shafts was crushed and dressed within the series of mills which utilized the same leat and the power for pumping was derived from a series of flat rods. The stamping mills and tinners' buildings lying adjacent to or within the streamworks probably date to an earlier period of exploitation. (After Mercer 1986.)*

Topographical considerations were uppermost among the reasons for the establishment of a gunpowder works at a remote location on the Cherry Brook in 1844. The hazardous nature of the industry meant that the isolation of the area combined with a plentiful supply of water for the mills were vital factors. A recent detailed survey of the complex has revealed a series of buildings, many of which were served by leats. These buildings lie scattered over the area to minimize loss of life in the event of a catastrophic accident at any one of the mills (**72**). Powder from the works was mainly transported off the moor to the slate quarries in Cornwall, although some was used in the local granite quarries and mines. In its heyday the powder works employed around 100 people and although many travelled from settlements around the fringes of the moor, others lived in nearby cottages. The community which grew supported a school and chapel. The invention of dynamite was a crushing blow and heralded the demise of the industry. The works closed around 1890.

Peat cutting, an activity known to have been important to the moorland economy since at least the medieval period, continued to flourish. The precise scale cannot be established with any certainty, although in the early part of the seventeenth century a royal courtier believed that 100,000 horse-loads of peat (representing between 10,000 and 15,000 tons) were being taken from the moor each year. Sadly, no evidence was provided to support this statistic. Of the large areas of peat-cutting earthworks, many probably date to this period. From the nineteenth century onwards, documentation makes it possible to be much more certain about the character of the industry. The digging of turves during the summer months for domestic use continued at a large number of locations. Also, a few large-scale

commercial operations were established. Foremost among these were the Walkham Head peatworks which supplied fuel for the mines at Mary Tavy, Blackbrook where peat was carried by tramway to the British Patent Naphtha Company works at Princetown, Red Lake which supplied peat to the naphtha works at Shipley Bridge, and Rattlebrook where various intermittent large-scale extraction operations lasted until the twentieth century.

In the nineteenth and twentieth centuries the largest impact on Dartmoor's landscape has been from forestry, the construction of reservoirs, military use and tourism. All four have substantially altered the appearance of the moor and together have damaged the archaeological resource bequeathed by earlier generations.

The first major forestry plantation was that at Fernworthy, where planting commenced soon after the First World War. Since this time at least 2000 hectares (4942 acres) have been incorporated into plantations. The largest of these include Bellever, Brimpts, Burrator, Canonteign, Laughter Hole and Soussons. Apart from the obvious change in the visual appearance of these areas, significant though varying damage has been caused to the

72 *The mill buildings forming the gunpowder works on the Cherry Brook. (Photograph Frances Griffith, Devon County Council: copyright reserved.)*

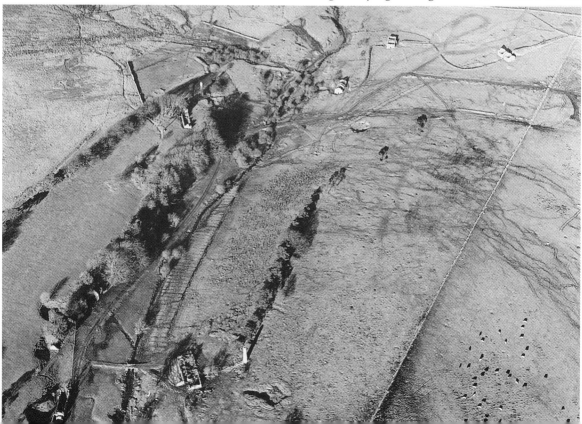

archaeology. In some instances individual monuments have not been planted upon, and in others the archaeology itself is robust enough to have escaped serious damage. However, in all instances their landscape context has been lost. In recent years more sympathetic management of these forests has generated both additional archaeological information and ensured the preservation of many of the surviving monuments.

The altitude of the moor results in an average rainfall of 2m (79in) per year and consequently there is an abundance of water. The first project designed to divert some of this from the moor to the growing town of Plymouth was in 1591 when the 29km (17mile) long Drakes Leat was constructed. This remarkable feat was made possible using the local skills of the tinners who surveyed and cut the leat. No reservoir was built to collect the water and this venture relied on the existing flow from the River Meavy. The second major extraction scheme was designed to carry water to Devonport and this too relied on weirs rather than reservoirs. The leat, known as the Devonport Leat, was completed by 1794 and collected over 9.1 million litres (2 million gallons) per day from the valleys of the West Dart, Cowsic and Blacka Brook.

The first reservoir to be constructed was at Tottiford in 1861, in response to a growing need for water in Torquay and Newton Abbot. Two further reservoirs were constructed within this area – one at Kennick in 1883 and another at Trenchford in 1907. In the south of the moor, Burrator was built to serve the growing population of Plymouth. The reservoir was completed in 1898 and originally held up to 3036 million litres (668 million gallons), though in later years the dam was heightened and its capacity increased to 4664 million litres (1026 million gallons). Increasing demands for water in other parts of Devon led to several additional reservoirs being built and among these are Venford (1907), Fernworthy (1942), Avon (1957) and Meldon (1970). Together, these reservoirs were

responsible for drowning significant areas of archaeological landscape, but at Burrator the adjoining farms were depopulated resulting in a well-preserved, fossilized late nineteenth-century agricultural landscape.

Intensive military use of Dartmoor for training purposes dates back to the 1880s when the War Department built its first permanent camp in Okehampton Park and leased an adjoining 51.80 square kilometres (20 square miles) from the Duchy of Cornwall. Since then, it has consolidated its presence and during the Second World War much of the area was used for training. The series of aerial photographs taken by the RAF during 1946 clearly illustrates the impact. Substantial camps at Okehampton, Willsworthy and Plaster Down, together with an airfield at Harrowbeer and rifle range at Rippon Tor, are among the most dramatic features. Closer examination of other parts of the moor indicate widespread activity. In the Merrivale area for example, a large number of small circular earthworks probably indicate mortar training. Today the most obvious visual impact of the military are the various targets, slit-trenches, tramways, roads, shell holes, and observation buildings.

The impact of tourism on the landscape is considerable. Since the nineteenth century Dartmoor has become an increasingly popular tourist destination. While this has undoubtedly increased awareness about protecting the area, it has also contributed to its changing character. At the most fundamental level, facilities such as car parks, toilets, roads and other facilities have all been developed to meet the needs of the visitor. The impact of over 10 million visitors to the moor each year on the archaeology are difficult to quantify, although examination of many of the more prominent monuments indicates damage and erosion, some at least of which is the result of visitor activity. The moor, however, remains essentially an agricultural landscape over which many thousands of animals graze as they have for generations.

7

The Dartmoor palimpsest

The complex archaeological landscape of Dartmoor has produced a palimpsest of features as it has evolved. The progressive alterations of successive generations have left indelible marks to bear witness to their passing. As indicated at the start of this book the archaeologist deciphers the palimpsest by removing layers of time, and in a sense peeling away those structures and artefacts which belong to each age. The preceding chapters have defined which types of site may be recognized in each period, to enable the reader to do the same when looking at any particular portion of Dartmoor. In this final chapter, a few selected areas of this diverse landscape have been specifically highlighted, in order to illustrate how this may be achieved.

The most effective method by which to present the information relating to the archaeological landscape, and so to begin to comprehend something of what is actually going on, is to produce a plan or map. Butler's Atlas of Antiquities currently represents the most complete readily available source of archaeological mapping for the moor, and in turning to any one of his sixty-five maps, the richness, diversity and complexity of the resource soon becomes apparent. In all likelihood, any plan will be a network of interconnecting walls, banks and ditches punctuated sporadically with buildings and structures of all ages. The simplest way to approach the palimpsest is to work from the present backwards. As you retreat through time you can begin to see the modern field boundaries and roads disappear, and without these the landscape

begins to change drastically. Looking for the types of sites known to date to specific periods, it is then possible to see the landscape 'undevelop', to become less complicated. The further back you go the less 'background noise' there will be until the only remaining features are geological and topographic, such as rivers and hillsides. Bearing in mind the social, economic, religious and ecological factors, which have all been alluded to in the previous chapters, one can at last begin to visualize the characteristic changes which have been wrought through time and the subsequent impact these have made on the landscape. Only when we comprehend the evolution can we appreciate the development.

To illustrate the complexity of palimpsests, the following four examples have been included for the reader to unravel experimentally. These I have named after the river valley in which each are situated: the Meavy, Plym, Walkham and Dart.

The Meavy
This landscape encompasses the upper part of the Meavy valley and may be divided into two distinct parts (**73**). On the lower ground, medieval and post-medieval fields, together with their settlements and tracks dominate a landscape itself now hidden partly by dense tree growth. In the valley bottoms are tin streamworks. On the higher ground, dispersed prehistoric round-house settlements survive together with their reaves, enclosures, cairns and stone rows. At the interface between these two distinct areas, archaeological

features belonging to both the prehistoric and later landscapes are found juxtaposed. Originally the prehistoric archaeology would have extended more fully into those areas dominated by the historic, but because of intensive re-use of these areas, the earlier archaeological picture has been almost completely erased. At the same time the historic landscape situated at the upper limits of its own distribution is also peripheral. Therefore, side by side are two totally different cultural responses to identical environmental conditions. This juxtaposition of well-preserved archaeology has much to offer those wishing to study the responses of different cultures to the same environment.

The Plym

In marked contrast to the situation in the Meavy valley, archaeological features of different dates are predominantly found intermixed within the Upper Plym valley and there is no obvious demarcation (**74**). At Legis Tor enclosures of prehistoric date contain later pillow mounds and vermin traps. On the western slopes of Trowlesworthy a post-medieval building lies within an earlier enclosure. At Hentor Warren a separate block of historic fields incorporates an earlier reave. The valley bottoms were extensively streamed for tin. Unusually, however, a small number of pillow mounds were constructed within the disused tinworks. The distribution of burial cairns is of interest. With the exception of those on Ringmoor Down, all the examples are situated close to round-house settlements, although their siting between such settlements may have been of particular significance to the inhabitants.

The Walkham

This section of the Walkham valley, to the north of Merrivale, includes discrete areas of intensive use (**75**). This landscape is predominantly a prehistoric one, although historic field systems and a small quantity of tinworking do encroach onto it. At Merrivale, a round-house settlement and ritual complex lie side by side. Leading through the area is the Great Western Reave – which at over 10 kilometres (6 miles) is the longest known territorial

reave on the moor. At Merrivale, the settlement appears to have slighted this impressive land division boundary, while within the vicinity of the Merrivale Newtake settlements and that below Roos Tor it is intact. This may suggest that the Merrivale settlement is of a different date to the other two. Other differences between the prehistoric settlements are obvious. Some consist of clusters of huts associated with irregular aggregate fields, others are partially enclosed. A small number are associated with cairnfields and a few appear to be relatively isolated and associated with neither enclosures nor fields. These differences may be chronological or represent differences in their economic character. Compared with the large number of prehistoric settlements, there are few historic ones and this is probably the major reason why the earlier landscape has been only partially altered.

The Dart

Substantial coaxial field-systems survive over large areas of the north-eastern side of the moor. The Dartmeet field-system covers an area of 3000 hectares and figure **76** shows only part of its

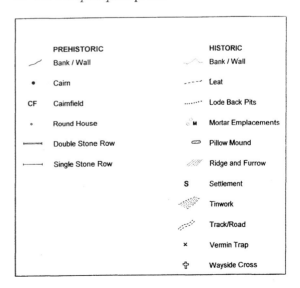

PREHISTORIC		HISTORIC	
/	Bank / Wall		Bank / Wall
•	Cairn	- - - -	Leat
CF	Cairnfield	....	Lode Back Pits
○	Round House	M	Mortar Emplacements
▬▬	Double Stone Row	⬠	Pillow Mound
▬	Single Stone Row	▨	Ridge and Furrow
		S	Settlement
			Tinwork
			Track/Road
		×	Vermin Trap
		✝	Wayside Cross

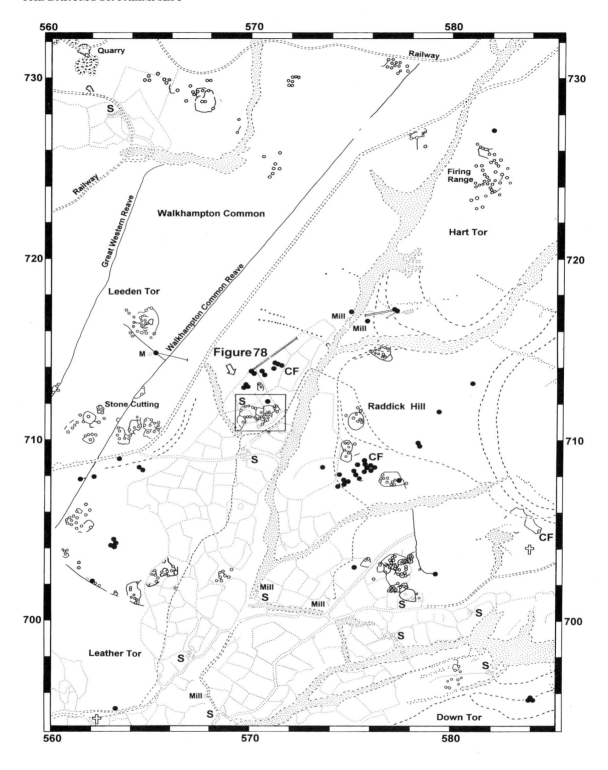

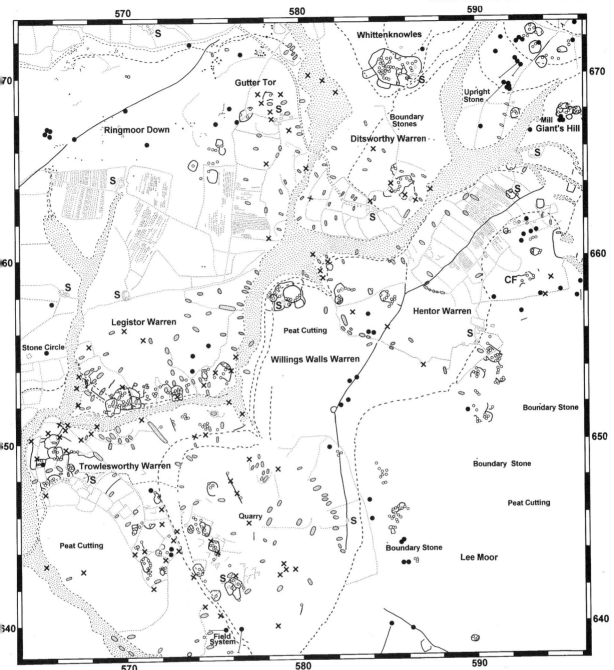

73 *The Meavy palimpsest. (Based upon the 1982 Ordnance Survey 1:10,000 map with the permission of The Controller of Her Majesty's Stationery Office: Crown copyright, Butler 1994 and Author.)*

74 *The Plym palimpsest. (Based upon the 1982 Ordnance Survey 1:10,000 map with the permission of The Controller of Her Majesty's Stationery Office: Crown copyright, Butler 1994, Mercer 1986 and Author.)*

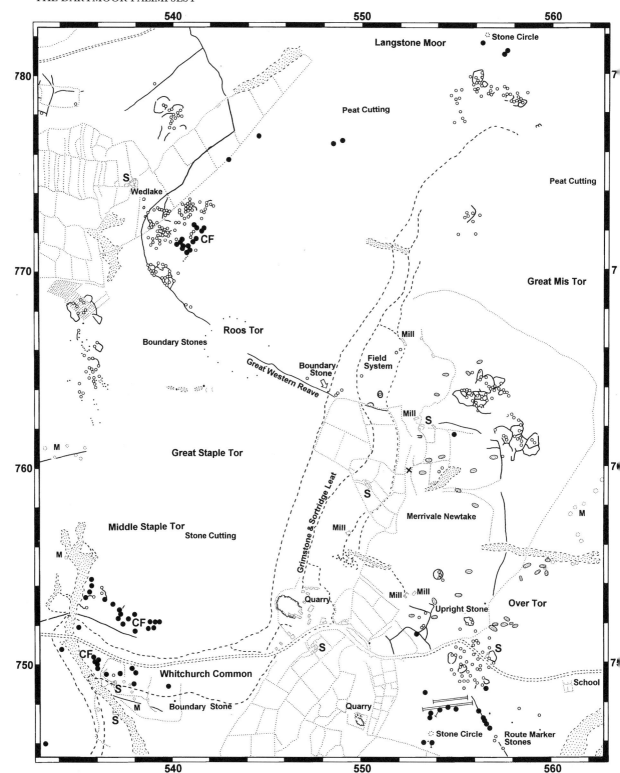

75 *The Walkham palimpsest. (Based upon the 1982 Ordnance Survey 1:10,000 map with the permission of The Controller of Her Majesty's Stationery Office: Crown copyright, Butler 1992 and Author.)*

76 *The Dart palimpsest. (Based upon the 1982 Ordnance Survey 1:10,000 map with the permission of The Controller of Her Majesty's Stationery Office: Crown copyright, Butler 1993 and Fleming 1988.)*

extent. A coaxial field-system dominates this area, its character still surviving in many of the adjacent historic fields. Compared with the large clusters of houses associated with the enclosures in the other areas, the settlements contain only a few houses, except at one point just beyond the terminal reave. Although the extensive system survives largely intact over large parts, in others it has been altered, damaged or obliterated by historic activity including farming and tinworking (**77**).

The four examples considered above each covers a relatively large area. The same principles can be used to study a smaller area or in some circumstances even an individual building. In assembling an overview of the landscape it is essential to build up from its basic components. Thus, the individual round house which started life as a timber building before being converted to a stone one is

77 *The complex character of the archaeological palimpsest on Holne Moor is highlighted by this photograph which shows only part of the area depicted in **76**.(RC8-HL105, Cambridge University Collection of Air Photographs: copyright reserved.)*

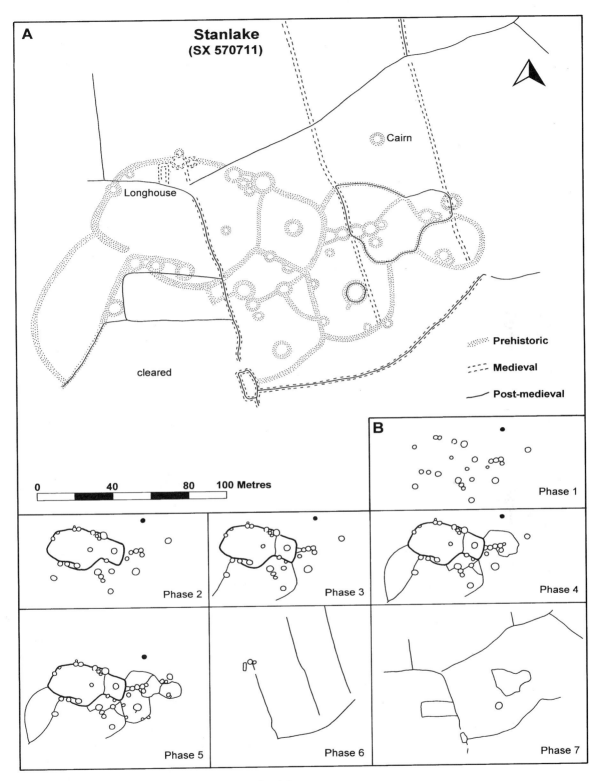

78 *A. Simplified plan of the complex palimpsest at Stanlake.*
B. Series of plans showing how this monument may have evolved. (Butler 1994 and Author.)

as much a part of the overall landscape as its fields. During successive generations of use, the building will undergo remodelling, enlargement, and perhaps modernization before finally being abandoned. This same building may then be re-used as a shelter or animal pen before being partly robbed to build a nearby wall. The landscape is dynamic, but without excavation or detailed survey archaeologists are only able to see the final product of this change. To illustrate this point it is worth looking at a site in the upper Meavy valley at Stanlake (**78**). Here, within a relatively small area, archaeological fieldwork has recorded a large prehistoric round-house settlement complete with simple and agglomerated enclosures and cairns, onto which a medieval longhouse settlement and field-systems were superimposed, before finally, in post-medieval times, the area became part of a more extensive field-system associated with the nearby farm of Stanlake. Archaeologically, though each successive generation has altered and in some instances destroyed traces of earlier activity, enough remains to enable the field archaeologist to untangle the different components and present a useful interpretation of the manner in which this small part of the moor developed through time.

To interpret this landscape it is crucial that the relative dates of the different features are established. The raw data to allow this work to be carried out are provided by detailed field survey which records the shape and position of the different features relative to each other (see **78**). During the survey care needs to be taken to ensure that the relationship between the different features is recorded and from this information it is possible to build up a picture. Clearly many features are not related to any others and in these circumstances the archaeologist needs to compare these features with others within the study area, or if necessary from outside, to provide the clues for their relative dates. The interpretative plan generated from the fieldwork at Stanlake is presented here, but the final result of this analysis is the reconstructions which express more clearly than words how archaeological information can be translated into a meaningful format (**colour plates 12, 13** and **14**).

All such work is necessarily coloured by current interpretations and attitudes to the past. The process of converting raw archaeological data into a documented format and finally into an interpretation is inevitably influenced to some extent by current preconceptions. The archaeological landscape presented in this book is necessarily a reflection of the impact that the ideas of earlier and contemporary scholars have had upon myself, and so it is clearly a personal approach.

In a work of this length it is not possible to examine in detail the landscape archaeology of an area with such a rich legacy as Dartmoor. Inevitably certain themes and areas of the moor have not received the attention they deserve and, at times, issues which still remain fiercely contested have had to be summarized in a manner which may not have done them justice. I hope, however, that it has been possible to describe, illustrate and explain – and most importantly to demonstrate – that on Dartmoor we are fortunate to have a well-preserved multi-period relict landscape capable of providing an insight into prehistoric and historic life. Past research has clearly generated much thought-provoking information and ideas, but many questions still remain unanswered. Future research must, and I am sure will, be directed towards developing fresh strategies designed to decipher and interpret the whole landscape.

Glossary

adit Used in mining, a horizontal tunnel driven into the hillside to facilitate access, drainage and haulage of ore to the surface.

cairn There are two major types of funerary cairn. Round cairns generally survive as circular stone and earth mounds, covering at least one burial. Ring cairns vary considerably in character but most consist of a ring-bank of stone and earth surrounding either an open area, mound or tor outcrop. Most cairns are considered to have been constructed during the Bronze Age though some may be Neolithic.

cairn cemetery A cluster of five or more funerary cairns.

cairnfields Areas where stone has been cleared and placed into heaps. Most cairnfields consist of more than ten circular or oval mounds and some contain at least one funerary cairn; however, they are generally associated with agricultural activity.

chambered tomb A long mound of stone and earth containing a chamber constructed from often massive stones, or megaliths, and of Neolithic date. The chamber was regularly opened to enable the interment of selected skeletal fragments. Also referred to as long cairns, cromlechs or portal dolmens.

cist A stone coffin. Most lie within or under a cairn, and are orientated approximately north-west to south-east. Some cists do not appear to be associated with a cairn, but in many of these instances the mound has probably been totally removed.

coaxial field-system Groups of fields arranged on a single prevailing axis, subdivided by transverse boundaries and demarcated by a terminal reave at either end.

enclosure An area surrounded by a wall or bank. Enclosures vary considerably in size, shape and date, although most of the circular ones are considered to be Bronze Age. Many contain round houses and may have been subdivided while others contain no visible structures. It is not uncommon to find enclosures attached to each other (agglomerated).

farmstead A single farmhouse together with outbuildings and ancillary structures.

hamlet A group of no more than six farmhouses clustered together. Occasionally there may also be a church, chapel, shop and workers' accommodation.

hillfort A strategically important hilltop position defended by single or multiple ramparts and ditches. Most hillforts were built during the Iron Age, and were occupied periodically in time of perceived crisis.

irregular aggregate field-system Groups of individually shaped fields which have developed in a haphazard manner through time.

leat An artificial channel to carry water.

lode A linear area of mineralization within the underground rock.

longhouse Through-passage, rectangular, dual-purpose building in which domestic and animal accommodation was provided under one roof.

lynchet Steep linear breaks in the slope formed by erosion and soil build-up caused by ploughing.

mortar stone A stone on which ore was crushed by mechanically driven stamps. The continual pounding of the stamps resulted in the formation of distinctive small saucer-shaped hollows.

microlith Small worked flint flakes and blades of Mesolithic date. Often originally used in conjunction with other materials such as wood and antler.

palimpsest This term is used metaphorically to describe a complex landscape which contains archaeological information dating to more than one period.

pillow mound Long flat-topped mound surrounded by a ditch. Beneath the mound interconnecting tunnels, capped with flat stones or turves, acted as artificial burrows for rabbits. The warrens on the moor each contain large numbers of pillow mounds, which are also known as buries.

reave A general term covering all types of linear prehistoric land boundary. They survive as banks of stone and earth. The dimensions of individual reaves vary considerably; some of the large territorial reaves extend over 10km (6 miles), while those within coaxial field-systems can be under 50m (51 yards) long.

ridge and furrow Series of low parallel banks and hollows, a consequence of cultivation, either by ploughing or, more occasionally, digging.

round house Structures, often referred to as hut circles, which generally survive as stone and earth walls surrounding a circular or oval internal area. Prehistoric in origin, many were dwellings,

although some of the smaller ones were undoubtedly ancillary buildings.

stannary A district under the jurisdiction of a legal and administrative organization, the Stannary Court, which passed laws, protected the privileges of tinners and supervised the collection of taxes on tin presented for coinage. The four stannary towns serving Devon were Ashburton, Chagford, Tavistock and Plympton.

stone circle A ring or rings of upright stones set around an open space. Most examples are considered to be Bronze Age although some may have had Neolithic origins.

stone row An alignment of one or more lines of upright stones set at intervals. Most rows are directly associated with cairns and located on the fringes of current moorland. They are presumed to be late Neolithic or Early Bronze Age in origin. Also referred to as stone alignments.

tin mill A building in which machinery powered by one or more waterwheels was used to process tin ore. Stamping and crazing mills crushed the ore and blowing mills smelted it.

tinwork A term which covers all the different types of tin extraction including streamworking and mining.

typology The classification of monuments based on similarities in form and character.

vermin trap Stone-built funnels which directed vermin into a centrally placed trap. Most rabbit warrens have traps, generally either X- or V-shaped, and most surviving examples are of post-medieval date.

Places to visit

Dartmoor itself is a large, complex, multi-period archaeological landscape and, consequently, a casual afternoon stroll anywhere within it will bring one into contact with relics from the past. There are, however, particular areas and monuments which illustrate more clearly the character, diversity and richness of this important landscape. Some of these have been selected and are presented below together with some brief details of what one might expect to see (**79**).

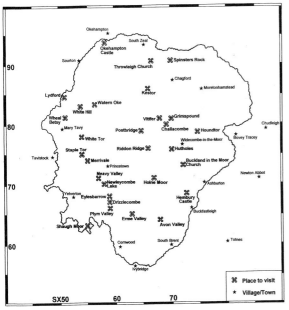

79 *Location of places to visit.*

Those wishing to make most of their visit to this rich archaeological landscape should obtain a copy of the 1:25,000 Ordnance Survey Outdoor Leisure Map No. 28. This depicts public access, military live-firing ranges, the character of the topography, as well as many of the archaeological monuments. This map does not, however, illustrate those parts of the moor which are covered in a dense blanket of bracken during the summer months. Many sites are totally invisible from June and this means that they can only really be appreciated during the spring when the previous season's growth has died back. All of the sites and areas suggested below are currently either wholly or largely accessible to the public, but the mention or depiction of a site or area within this book does not necessarily mean that there is public access. Many of the monuments described and illustrated within this book are protected under the Ancient Monuments and Archaeological Areas Act 1979 and it is an offence to damage or interfere with them. The purpose of this legislation is to ensure that future generations may continue to visit, enjoy and study the moor's archaeology.

Together with brief details of the sites, an Ordnance Survey grid reference is included and, where appropriate, illustration figure numbers are given in bold type. No details of routes are provided since many of the sites have several possible starting points.

Avon Valley, upper (SX 6864) (**21, 25, 27, 28, 29, 44** and **59**)
Within this valley lie the well-preserved remains of at least fourteen enclosed settlements including Rider's Rings and the excavated site on Dean Moor. Other monuments of prehistoric date include a stone row on Black Tor and around thirty cairns elsewhere within the area. Rabbit warrens of historic date survive at Black Tor and Huntingdon, while many lengths of the valley bottom contain the earthworks from tin streaming. Cutting into the valley sides are several openworks and other evidence of tinworking includes tin mills and shelters.

St Peter's Church, Buckland in the Moor
(SX 72047314)
This twelfth-century church was rebuilt in the fifteenth

century when a magnificent rood screen featuring a series of painted panels was added.

Challacombe (SX 692800) (**48** and **colour plate 1**)
The scale and character of this medieval field-system is best appreciated from the hillside opposite, and in particular when visiting Grimspound it can be seen extending along the hillside.

Drizzlecombe (SX 5967) (**19, 33** and **74**)
Three stone rows together with at least twenty cairns lie immediately next to a large, partially enclosed, stone round-house settlement.

Erme Valley, upper (SX 6365) (**16, 25, 28, 29, 33** and **59**)
Both sides of this valley contain abundant evidence of prehistoric settlement and ritual. At least 400 round houses are known to survive together with over 120 enclosures many of which are agglomerated. The longest stone row on Dartmoor runs south for 3320m (3632 yards) from Green Hill and several other well-preserved examples, as well as over 100 cairns, can be visited. Fine examples of tin streamworking earthworks survive in the valley bottoms, together with at least six tin mills and over thirty tinners' buildings.

Eylesbarrow (SX 5968) (**71**)
Earthworks and structures associated with nineteenth-century and earlier tin mining are scattered over the hillside in this area. Of particular interest is the series of six stamping mills and a smelting house which each utilized the same leat.

Grimspound (SX 700809) (**21, 28** and **colour plates 1** and **5**)
This partially enclosed stone round-house settlement is amongst the most visited on the moor. The main enclosure has substantial walls and some of the huts were reconstructed by the Dartmoor Exploration Committee. The medieval field-system lynchets at Challacombe are clearly visible from this monument.

Hembury Castle (SX 726684) (**41**)
Within woodland owned by the National Trust stands an Iron Age hillfort. This fort was re-fortified in the medieval period when a castle was established here. A small motte was constructed within the western part of the hillfort's interior and the original defences were probably remodelled to provide a substantial bailey.

Holne Moor (SX 6771) (**7, 16, 21, 49, 76** and **77**)
The southern part of the Dartmeet coaxial field-system can be examined here, together with a large number of round houses, a stone row and cairns. From the historic period, a farmstead, fields, several pillow mounds, a wayside cross, and evidence of tinworking including lode-back pits and streamworks, are all visible.

Houndtor (SX 746787) (**44** and **colour plate 8**)
The medieval settlements at Hound Tor were excavated by Minter in the 1960s. Today the larger settlement gives a good idea of the character of a medieval hamlet, while the smaller one at SX 745791 represents a typical farmstead. Both settlements are surrounded by contemporary fields, which are covered in dense bracken during the summer months.

Hutholes (SX 701758) (**44** and **colour plate 2**)
This well-preserved medieval settlement also excavated by Minter is now managed by the National Park which have provided a useful interpretative board.

Kestor (SX 6686) (**19, 21** and **38**)
An extensive area of coaxial field-system together with associated round houses including the Round Pound lie adjacent to several stone rows and a stone circle on Shovel Down.

Lydford (SX 509847) (**42** and **50**)
Two castles, the church dedicated to St Petrock, parts of the Anglo-Saxon burh defences and the fossilized street plan are still clearly visible within this small town.

Meavy Valley, upper (SX 5771) (**16, 24, 26, 32, 57, 59, 66, 73, 78** and **colour plates 12, 13** and **14**)
At least fifteen discrete prehistoric settlements, together with large numbers of funerary cairns, three cairn-fields, at least seven stone rows and a territorial reave provide evidence of an intensively exploited prehistoric landscape. The prehistoric settlement at Stanlake is well worth a visit, though it is densely covered in bracken during the summer months. The alluvial tin streamwork below this settlement is also worth visiting as are the stamping mills at Black Tor Falls.

Merrivale (SX 5574) (**10, 19, 28, 38, 75** and **colour plate 6**)
Four stone rows, seven cairns, a stone circle and standing stone lie adjacent to a partially enclosed, stone round-house settlement and the Great Western Reave.

Newleycombe Lake (SX 5870) (**18, 19, 29, 32, 33, 57** and **66**)
Tinworks of different types and date can be seen throughout this valley, which also contains a complex

post-medieval field-system which is clearly derived from a much earlier one.

Okehampton Castle (SX 58359426) (**50**)
This castle consists of a rectangular keep, built upon an earth mound (motte), with an elongated bailey containing the great hall, kitchen block, chapel and lodgings. Access to the bailey was through two gatehouses linked by a long, narrow passage. Most of the surviving fabric dates to the early fourteenth century though part of the keep is considered to be of Norman origin.

Plym Valley, upper (SX 5966) (**16, 28, 29, 33, 38, 59, 62, 63, 66** and **74**)
This valley contains a rich diversity of archaeological monuments belonging to the three major periods of activity represented on the moor. Particularly well-preserved prehistoric settlements exist on the southern slopes of Legis Tor, the western slopes of Trowlesworthy Tor, within Willings Walls Warren and at Whittenknowles Rocks. Leading through the area is the Willings Walls Warren contour reave which at certain points has been rebuilt in historic times. Archaeology of historic date is also abundant, with five warrens, several medieval settlements, their field systems and tinworks.

Postbridge (SX 64817890) (**64**)
This medieval clapper bridge consists of three spans resting on two piers and is considered by many to be the best-preserved example in Devon.

Riddon Ridge (SX 6676) (**31**)
The most extensive irregular aggregate field system on the Moor.

Shaugh Moor (SX 5563)
Beyond the coaxial field-system is a dispersed, partially enclosed, prehistoric settlement.

Spinsters' Rock (SX 70099078) (**14**)
This is the only chambered tomb with a complete chamber. Although reconstructed, it does give an idea of the impressive scale of these Neolithic monuments.

Staple Tor (SX 5475) (**67**)
Scattered around the slopes of Staple Tor are over 100 'sett-makers bankers'. These are stone benches on which stone hewn from the nearby surface rocks, was cut to make setts for road surfaces.

Throwleigh Church (SX 66769078) (**52**)
Much of the visible fabric of the Church of St Mary the Virgin dates to the fifteenth century, although the elaborately carved priest's door is probably of Norman origin. Enter the churchyard through a thatched lychgate attached to one side of the Tudor Church House and the shaft of a cross can be found to the left.

Vitifer (SX 6881)
The densest concentration of openworks on the moor is found within this area. In the bottoms of many are shafts associated with eighteenth- and nineteenth-century mining, and scattered around the area are numerous wheelpits which powered the mine at different times. The mine buildings, which include the dressing floors, a carpenter's shop, a blacksmith's shop, miners' 'dry', dormitory, kitchen, canteen, mine captain's house and other buildings, survive as foundations only.

Watern Oke (SX 564834) (**23**)
This Bronze Age settlement is not readily accessible, lying as it does some 3km (1¾ miles) from a road and within the military live-firing area. Its setting and sheer size makes one wonder at the character of the people who lived and worked in this remote, but beautiful spot.

Wheal Betsy (SX 51028138) (**colour plate 11**)
This well-preserved engine house lies immediately next to the A386, 2km (1¼ miles) north-north-east of Mary Tavy.

White Hill (SX 5383) (**32** and **37**)
A linear cairn cemetery and three cairnfields lying within the Willsworthy Range can only be visited when live firing is not taking place.

White Tor (SX 5478) (**13, 16, 31** and **37**)
On the summit of this hill is an enclosure considered to be of Neolithic date. On the slopes of this hill are a stone row, possible chambered tomb, a large number of cairns, seven Bronze Age settlements and a coaxial field-system leading off from the Great Western Reave.

Further reading

General

BUTLER, J., *Dartmoor Atlas of Antiquities. Volume 1 – The East*, Devon Books, 1991a.

BUTLER, J., *Dartmoor Atlas of Antiquities. Volume 2 – The North*, Devon Books, 1991b.

BUTLER, J., *Dartmoor Atlas of Antiquities. Volume 3 – The South-West*, Devon Books, 1994.

BUTLER, J., *Dartmoor Atlas of Antiquities. Volume 4 – The South-East*, Devon Books, 1993.

CROSSING, W., *Crossing's Guide to Dartmoor*, facsimile of 1912 edition, 1990, Peninsula Press.

FOX, A., *South West England*, Thames and Hudson, 1964.

GILL, C., *Dartmoor: A New Study*, David & Charles, 1970.

GRIFFITH, F., *Devon's Past – An Aerial View*, Devon Books, 1988.

HARRIS, H., *Industrial Archaeology of Dartmoor*, 3rd edition, David & Charles, 1986.

PAGE, J. L. W., *An Exploration of Dartmoor and its Antiquities*, Seeley & Co., 1889.

PEARCE, S., *The Archaeology of South-West Britain*, William Collins, 1981.

THURLOW, G., *Thurlow's Dartmoor Companion*, Peninsula Press, 1993.

TODD, M., *A Regional History of England: The South-West to A.D. 1000*, Longmans, 1987.

WOODS, S. H., *Dartmoor Stone*, Devon Books, 1988.

WORTH, R. H., *Worth's Dartmoor*, 3rd impression, David & Charles, 1981.

Landscape interpretation

ATKINSON, N., *Dartmoor National Park Plan: Second Review 1991*, Dartmoor National Park, 1991.

BECKETT, S. C., 'Pollen analysis of the peat deposits' in Smith, K., Coppen, J., Wainwright, G. J. and Beckett, S., 'The Shaugh Moor Project: Third Report – settlement and environmental investigation', *Proceedings Prehistoric Society*, no. 47, 1981, pp. 245–66.

GERRARD, S., 'The Dartmoor tin industry: an archaeo-logical perspective', in 'The archaeology of Dartmoor – Perspectives from the 1990s', *Devon Archaeological Society Proceedings*, no. 52, 1994, 173–98.

MERCER, R. J., *An Archaeological Field Survey of the Upper Plym Valley, Dartmoor 1982–1986*, unpublished report by Edinburgh Archaeological Services on behalf of English Heritage, 1986.

Hunter-fisher-gatherers

CASELDINE, C. J. and MAGUIRE, D. J., 'A review of the prehistoric and historic environment on Dartmoor', *Devon Archaeological Society Proceedings*, no. 39, 1981, pp. 1–16.

JACOBI, R., 'Early Flandrian hunters in the South-West', *Devon Archaeological Society Proceedings*, no. 37, 1979, pp. 48–93.

SIMMONS, I. G., 'An outline of the vegetation history of Dartmoor', *Rep. Trans. Devonshire Ass.*, no. 94, 1962, pp. 555–74.

STAINES, S., 'Environmental change on Dartmoor', *Devon Archaeological Society Proceedings*, no. 37, 1979, pp. 21–47.

Neolithic Dartmoor

EMMETT, D. D., 'Stone rows: the traditional view reconsidered', *Devon Archaeological Society Proceedings*, no. 37, 1979, pp. 94–114.

EOGAN, G. and SIMMONS, I. G., 'The excavation of a stone alignment and circle at Cholwichtown, Lee Moor, Devonshire', *Proceedings Prehistoric Society*, no. 30, 1964, pp. 25–38.

FLETCHER, M., GRINSELL, L. V. and QUINNELL, N. V., 'A long cairn on Butterdon Hill, Ugborough', *Devon Archaeological Society Proceedings*, no. 32, 1974a, pp. 163–4.

TURNER, J. R., 'Chamber cairns, Gidleigh', *Devon Archaeological Society Proceedings*, no. 38, 1980, pp. 117–19.

Bronze Age Dartmoor

ANDERSON, I. K., 'Eleventh Report of the Dartmoor Exploration Committee' *Rep. Trans. Devonshire Ass.*, no. 38, 1906, pp. 101–13.

BARING-GOULD, S., BURNARD, R., WORTH, R. N., WORTH, R. H., ROWE, J. B., PODE, J. D. and BERRY, G. B., 'Second Report of the Dartmoor Exploration Committee', *Rep. Trans. Devonshire Ass.*, no. 27, 1895, pp. 81–92.

BARING-GOULD, S., BURNARD, R., ROWE, J. B., PODE, J. D. and WORTH, R. H., 'Fifth Report of the Dartmoor Exploration Committee', *Rep. Trans. Devonshire Ass.*, no. 30, 1898, pp. 97–115.

BARING-GOULD, S., 'Fourth Report of the Dartmoor Exploration Committee', *Rep. Trans. Devonshire Ass.*, no. 29, 1897, pp. 145–65.

BURL, A., *The Stone Circles of the British Isles*, Yale University Press, 1976.

COLLIS, J., 'Field systems and boundaries on Shaugh Moor and at Wotter, Dartmoor', *Devon Archaeological Society Proceedings*, no. 41, 1983, pp. 47–61.

FLEMING, A., 'The prehistoric landscape of Dartmoor. Part 1: South Dartmoor', *Proceedings Prehistoric Society*, no. 44, 1978, pp. 97–123.

FLEMING, A., 'The Dartmoor reaves: boundary patterns and behaviour patterns in the second millennium BC', *Devon Archaeological Society Proceedings*, no. 37, 1979, pp. 115–50.

FLEMING, A., 'The cairnfields of North-West Dartmoor', *Devon Archaeological Society Proceedings*, no. 38, 1980, pp. 9–12.

FLEMING, A., 'The prehistoric landscape of Dartmoor. Part 2: North and East Dartmoor', *Proceedings Prehistoric Society*, no. 49, 1983, pp. 195–241.

FLEMING, A., *The Dartmoor Reaves – Investigating Prehistoric Land Divisions*, 1st edition, Batsford, 1988.

FLETCHER, M., GRINSELL, L. V. and QUINNELL, N. V., 'A stone circle on Mardon Down, Moretonhampstead', *Devon Archaeological Society Proceedings*, no. 32, 1974b, pp. 164–6.

FOX, A., 'Excavations on Dean Moor, in the Avon Valley, 1954–1956', *Rep. Trans. Devonshire Ass.*, no. 89, 1957, pp. 18–77.

GAWNE, E., 'Field patterns in Widecombe Parish and the Forest of Dartmoor', *Rep. Trans. Devonshire Ass.*, no. 102, 1970, pp. 49–69.

GAWNE, E., and COCKS, J. V. S., 'Parallel reaves on Dartmoor', *Rep. Trans. Devonshire Ass.*, no. 100, 1968, pp. 277–91.

GRINSELL, L. V., 'Dartmoor Barrows', *Devon Archaeological Society Proceedings*, no. 36, 1978, pp. 85–180.

HAMOND, F., 'Settlement, economy and environment on prehistoric Dartmoor', *Devon Archaeological Society Proceedings*, no. 37, 1979, pp. 146–75.

PENHALLURICK, R. D., *Tin in Antiquity*, The Institute of Metals, 1986.

PETTIT, P., *Prehistoric Dartmoor*, David & Charles, 1974.

RADFORD, C. A. R., 'Prehistoric settlement on Dartmoor and the Cornish moors', *Proceedings Prehistoric Society*, no. 18, 1952, pp. 55–84.

TURNER, J. R., 'Ring cairns, stone circles and related monuments on Dartmoor', *Devon Archaeological Society Proceedings*, no. 48, 1990, pp. 27–86.

WAINWRIGHT, G. J. and SMITH, K., 'The Shaugh Moor Project: Second Report – The Enclosure', *Proceedings Prehistoric Society*, no. 46, 1980, pp. 65–122.

Dartmoor's dark ages: Iron Age to Early Christian Era

ADDYMAN, P. V., In Wilson, D. M. and Hurst, D. G 'Medieval Britain in 1965', *Medieval Archaeology*, no. 10, 1966, pp. 196–7.

COLLIS, J., 'Cranbrook Castle, Moretonhampstead, Devon. A new survey', *Devon Archaeological Society Proceedings*, no. 30, 1972, pp. 216–21.

EARL, B., 'Tin smelting at Week Ford, Dartmoor: a brief note', *Journal of the Historical Metallurgical Society*, no. 23, 1989, p. 119.

FOX, A., 'Excavations at Kestor: an early Iron Age settlement near Chagford, Devon', *Rep. Trans. Devonshire Ass.*, no. 86, 1954, pp. 21–62.

GIBSON, A., 'The excavation of an Iron Age settlement at Gold Park, Dartmoor', *Devon Archaeological Society Proceedings*, no. 50, 1992, pp. 19–46.

PEARCE, S., 'Early medieval land use on Dartmoor and its flanks', *Devon Archaeology*, no. 3, 1985, pp. 13–19.

SILVESTER, R. J., 'The relationship of first millennium settlement to the upland areas of the South West', *Devon Archaeological Society Proceedings*, no. 37, 1979, pp. 176–90.

SILVESTER, R. J. and QUINNELL, N. V., 'Unfinished hillforts on the Devon Moors', *Devon Archaeological Society Proceedings*, no. 51, 1993, pp. 17–31.

Medieval Dartmoor

AUSTIN, D., 'Excavations in Okehampton Deer Park, Devon 1976–1978', *Devon Archaeological Society Proceedings*, no. 36, 1978, pp. 191–239.

AUSTIN, D., 'Dartmoor and the upland village of the south-west of England', in Hooke, D., ed., *Medieval Villages*, Oxford University Committee for Archaeology, monograph no. 5, 1985, pp. 71–9.

AUSTIN, D., DAGGETT, R. H. and WALKER, M. J. C., 'Farms and fields in Okehampton Park, Devon', *Landscape History*, no. 2, 1980, pp. 39–58.

BEACHAM, P., 'The Dartmoor longhouse', *Devon Archaeology*, no. 3, 1985, pp. 23–30.

BERESFORD, G., 'Three deserted medieval settlements on Dartmoor: a report on the late E. Marie Minters' excavations', *Medieval Archaeology*, no. 23, 1979, pp. 98–158.

CHERRY, B. and PEVSNER, N., *The Buildings of England – Devon*, 2nd revised edition, Penguin Books, 1989.

CROSSING, W., *The ancient stone crosses of Dartmoor and its borderland*, facsimile edition, Devon Books, 1987.

FLEMING, A. and RALPH, N., 'Medieval settlement and land use on Holne Moor, Dartmoor: the landscape evidence', *Medieval Archaeology*, no. 26, 1982, pp. 101–37.

FOX, A., 'A monastic settlement on Dean Moor, South Devon', *Medieval Archaeology*, no. 2, 1958, pp. 141–57.

HIGHAM, R. A., ALLAN, J. P. and BLAYLOCK, S. R., 'Excavations at Okehampton Castle, Devon. Part 2: The bailey', *Devon Archaeological Society Proceedings*, no. 40, 1982, pp. 19–151.

LINEHAN, C. D., 'Deserted sites and rabbit-warrens on Dartmoor, Devon', *Medieval Archaeology*, no. 10, 1966, pp. 113–44.

SAUNDERS, A. D., 'Lydford Castle', *Medieval Archaeology*, no. 24, 1980, pp. 123–86.

STARKEY, F. H., *Dartmoor Crosses and some Ancient Tracks*, 2nd edition, F. H. Starkey, 1989.

Post-medieval Dartmoor

HAYNES, R. G., 'Ruined Sites on Dartmoor' (undated and unpublished, ms. in Plymouth Museum).

HEMERY, E., *Walking The Dartmoor Railroads*, Reprint, Peninsula Press, 1991.

LE MESSURIER, B., 'The Phillpotts peat passes of Northern Dartmoor – a pioneer survey', *Rep. Trans. Devonshire Ass.*, no. 97, 1965, pp. 161–70.

LE MESSURIER, B., 'The post-prehistoric structures of central north Dartmoor – a field survey', *Rep. Trans. Devonshire Ass.*, no. 111, 1979, pp. 59–73.

NEWMAN, P., 'The Moorland Meavy – a tinners' landscape', *Rep. Trans. Devonshire Ass.*, no. 119, 1987, pp. 223–40.

Index

General

The Author

Dr Sandy Gerrard is Monuments Protection Programme Archaeologist for English Heritage on Dartmoor. He has directed major excavations on Bodmin Moor and in Pembrokeshire, carried out extensive fieldwork throughout south-west Britain, and lives in Devon, where he keeps poultry and goats.

England contains an extraordinary mosaic of discrete landscapes, each with its own distinct topography, geology, settlement history – and archaeology. They are the most eloquent witnesses of England's complex rural history. The Landscapes books in this series enable the reader to see history in landscape. Each describes the total archaeology of a particular landscape, from prehistory to the industrial past.

Professor Graeme Barker,
General Editor, Landscapes books

'One of the great classic series of British archaeology.' *Current Archaeology*

This volume is part of a major series, jointly conceived for English Heritage and Batsford, under the general editorship of Dr Stephen Johnson at English Heritage.

Titles in the series:

Sites
Avebury Caroline Malone
Danebury Barry Cunliffe
Dover Castle Jonathan Coad
Flag Fen: Prehistoric Fenland Centre Francis Pryor
Fountains Abbey Glyn Coppack
Glastonbury Philip Rahtz
Hadrian's Wall Stephen Johnson
Housesteads James Crow
Ironbridge Gorge Catherine Clark
Lindisfarne Deirdre O'Sullivan and Robert Young
Maiden Castle Niall M. Sharples
Roman Bath Barry Cunliffe
Roman London Gustav Milne
Roman York Patrick Ottaway
Stonehenge Julian Richards
Tintagel Charles Thomas
The Tower of London Geoffrey Parnell
Viking Age York Richard Hall
Wharram Percy: Deserted Medieval Village Maurice Beresford and John Hurst
Forthcoming
St Augustine's Abbey Richard Gem et al.

Periods
Anglo-Saxon England Martin Welch
Bronze Age Britain Michael Parker Pearson
Industrial England Michael Stratton and Barrie Trinder
Iron Age Britain Barry Cunliffe
Roman Britain Martin Millett
Viking Age England Julian D. Richards
Forthcoming
Norman England Trevor Rowley
Stone Age Britain Nick Barton

Subjects
Abbeys and Priories Glyn Coppack
Canals Nigel Crowe
Castles Tom McNeill
Channel Defences Andrew Saunders
Church Archaeology Warwick Rodwell
Life in Roman Britain Joan Alcock
Prehistoric Settlements Robert Bewley
Roman Towns in Britain Guy de la Bédoyère
Roman Villas and the Countryside Guy de la Bédoyère
Shrines and Sacrifice Ann Woodward
Victorian Churches James Stevens Curl
Forthcoming
Roman Forts in Britain Paul Bidwell
Seaside Architecture Simon H. Adamson
Ships and Shipwrecks Peter Marsden

Towns
Canterbury Marjorie Lyle
Chester Peter Carrington
Durham Martin Roberts
Norwich Brian Ayers
Winchester Tom Beaumont James
York Richard Hall

Landscapes
Dartmoor Sandy Gerrard
The Peak District John Barnatt and Ken Smith
Forthcoming
The Cotswolds Timothy Darvill and Alan McWhirr
The Yorkshire Dales Robert White